Sampler of the

Miraculous Interventions™ Series

by Deborah Aubrey-Peyron

with bonus preview of
"Christmas Chaos!"
by Deborah Aubrey-Peyron

Home Crafted Artistry & Printing
New Albany, IN 47150

Sampler of the

Miraculous Interventions™ *Series*

by Deborah Aubrey-Peyron

with bonus preview of
"*Christmas Chaos!*"
by Deborah Aubrey-Peyron

Home Crafted Artistry & Printing
1252 Beechwood Avenue, New Albany, IN 47150

Contact information:
e-mail: HomeCraftedArtistry@yahoo.com
e-mail: peyronsinjesus@yahoo.com
Cover design by Mary Dow Bibb Smith
Photographs are author's family photos.

6

"...whatsoever ye do,

do all to the glory of God."

I Cor 10:31b KJV

TABLE OF CONTENTS . . 8

"**The Lord** shall establish thee
an holy people unto Himself,
as he hath sworn unto thee,
if thou shalt keep the commandments
of the Lord thy God,
and walk in His ways."
Deuteronomy 28: 9

"And as ye go, preach, saying,
the kingdom of heaven is at hand.
Heal the sick, cleanse the lepers,
raise the dead, cast out devils;
freely ye have received,
freely give."
Matthew 10: 7,8

"Behold, I will send my messenger,
and he shall prepare the way
before me...."
Malachi 3:1

"If you don't see miracles,
just adjust your vision."
Deb Peyron

Miraculous Interventions™

By

Deborah Aubrey-Peyron
With Contributions
by: Mark Peyron and Ben Merk

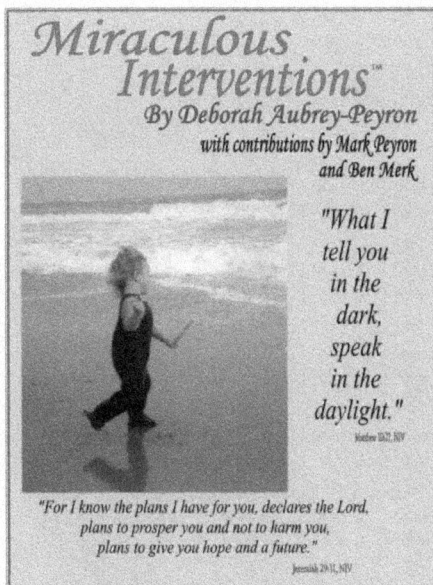

Miraculous
Interventions™
By Deborah Aubrey-Peyron
with contributions by Mark Peyron
and Ben Merk

"What I
tell you
in the
dark,
speak
in the
daylight."

Matthew 10:27, NIV

"For I know the plans I have for you, declares the Lord,
plans to prosper you and not to harm you,
plans to give you hope and a future."

Jeremiah 29:11, NIV

*True life
stories of
miraculous
events that
have
shaped the
author's life
and those
she has
known.*

PROLOGUE

Jesus forgave then he healed. Just as His Father does. See here, in Psalms 103:2-3 "Bless the Lord, O my soul, and forget not all His benefits: Who forgiveth all thine iniquities; who healeth all thy diseases." Mark 5:34 "And he said unto her, *Daughter, thy faith has made thee whole; go in peace, and be whole of thy plague.*"

Peace on the inside of the body can bring peace to the outside of the body.

I understand in the natural course of events of life we all get sick, but don't we sit above the natural? It's not the question of whether we get sick, but whether we have that faith or rapport with God to know He will bring us from the midst of this. For example, when my heart was healed of hate for my first husband, it wasn't six months before I met Mark, my husband now. I had to be healed of my past before I could move on to my future. Healing had to come.

Healing comes in many forms. It can be anything from a broken heart or a broken bone to a broken pocket book. Nothing is too hard for God!

Jesus called for all to be healed, and preach the gospel with signs and wonders. Your healing is the first sign and wonder to testify to. It is your confession.

These are mine.

A WILLING HEART
- MIKIE

While in the little house on Strawberry Lane, our two month old baby Andy came down very sick with Bronchialitis and RSV complications. He was quickly admitted to the *PICU at Audubon Hospital for eight days.

Shortly after coming home, the doctor ordered a bronchial nebulizer to administer breathing treatments several times a day for Andy until his lungs were fully healed. At that time, we had two babies in diapers and a five year old. Clarence was still making poverty wages for a family this size. Our car was very old and had no heat. When we would all have to go somewhere we wrapped everyone in blankets.

One week, it just wasn't enough. There was no way to make our money stretch. There was no gas in the car to take the baby to the doctor, no diaper money, and no money for needed medication.

The boys and I had run errands to the grocery on food stamps. When we got home I fixed lunch for Ben, age five and David, 20 months old. I made a cup of tea for myself and sat down to nurse Andy. While sitting, I added up in my head the bare essential money we needed for that day. It came up to $40.00.

I started crying. I told God that I had done all I knew how to do. Could He please find a way to give us $40.00. I had just finished burping the baby when I heard a knock on the door.

It was Clarence's cousin, Michael (Mikie). He was on his way to work just down the street from us. He said hello and inquired if we were okay or if we needed anything. I started to answer him when he said, "Wait, it doesn't matter. Here is $40.00."

I gasped and asked him, "How did you know we needed $40.00?"

He replied, "My God told me."

Of course He did.

PICU stands for Pediatric Intensive Care Unit

16

EPHESIANS 6:10-18
"THE ARMOR OF GOD"

By the time I was 35, my marriage to Clarence was over. I was separated and working at a bank in Louisville, Kentucky. Being a new hire, I went in to work sick with the flu. It was going around the office. I thought at that time, if you got sick, you just got sick. You had to wait for the doctor's medicine to heal you.

I had a temperature of over 101 degrees and felt awful! I called my doctor, who couldn't see me because he was so busy seeing other patients with the flu! It was then that I called my boys' pediatrician to see if she could see me. Her office was busy with the flu too! Her nurse, Vicki, who was a strong Christian said, "Debbie, let's pray together, you believe in Jesus." She prayed Ephesians 6:10-18, the armor of God, and that the blood of Christ would wash over me and heal me. She knew I would be healed.

By the time she finished praying, my temperature, aches, and pains, all left me. I was instantly healed! This was the first time I was ever made aware of instant healing. "Wow! Does anybody else know about this?" I thanked her so much and hung up ready to go back to work.

I took my cup of tea upstairs back to my desk and back to work. I went back among all those sick people, and I never caught as much as a sniffle.

Amen and amen!

Even illness has to bow to the name of Jesus!

MANNA FROM HEAVEN

In the spring of 1999, I went to school for medical assisting. The government was paying for our apartment for the three boys and myself, for me to go to school and our food stamps. I am still very grateful for all the help from those services. One month I ran short of food a couple of days early. I had a tendency to feed other kids in the housing complex. I must have over extended that month because our food supply did not go as far as usual.

That morning all I had to feed my sons was a can of what I called "who hash," and eight saltines. We were all so sad. For the first time, I had let my children down. I told the boys to go outside and play. I needed to go before the Lord in prayer. While praying, I felt in my spirit that I needed to ask my boyfriend, Mark, for $5.00. At that time, I could buy a package of hamburger, a loaf of bread, six apples, and a jar of peanut butter for that amount. You know, the good old days. The boys could have school breakfast for free.

Mark showed up 45 minutes later, and I wondered what took so long. He gave me $5.00 and said he would watch the boys until I got back. I thanked him very much and started for the store. I stopped by the front office of our complex to ask a question and saw that there were loaves of bread on the table out front. They had free bread! I asked if I could have two loaves, telling them what was going on in my life. They said, "Sure!"

While I was out believing and thanking God for the $5.00 and now the bread, God was working His real miracles, His favor. His five loaves and two fishes.

After I left the office the girls were upset! These people needed food! They called three church ministries who started packing up groceries and cash right away!

In the meantime, Mark was unpacking $70.00 worth of groceries out of his trunk into our apartment. That's what had taken so long. While he was there, Clarence, my ex-husband called the apartment. Mark answered the phone. He told Clarence we didn't have any food! Clarence told him he would go straight away to the grocery too and be right over! He brought in $40.00 worth of groceries.

I got back from the store thinking how wonderful God was to have given me the $5.00 and two loaves of bread to get us through. I walked through my front door and there was all this food in the kitchen that Mark brought. Clarence showed up 30 minutes later with his help! Then the three churches showed with food, toiletries and enough cash for gas in the car to last a month! There was also a pizza so big we couldn't close the oven door completely to cook it! The boys and I laughed and cried. I had a big kitchen, and you couldn't get all the food in the cabinets, on the counters and the kitchen table. It spilled out into the dining room!

So the next time you ask God for a little bit of help, open your arms wide!

WAIT FOR IT!

After my divorce from Clarence, my boys and I still managed to do nice things. We went on a few trips, vacations, day excursions to the local amusement park in the summer and fall, picnics and family nights. We made joyful times to help us all heal. When my boys were growing up, the amusement park in the summer was their favorite place to go! I'd make sandwiches and drinks, and off we'd go, over the river to the city for a day of fun in the sun at the pool, park and rides.

We'd usually start pool side where it wasn't so crowded. The boys would race around the Lazy River. I would paddle and take my time, relaxing. There was a strong undercurrent that kept the water flowing around the river. When you got to the area where you got out, the current was strong enough to knock a person over if you were not careful.

While I was still going around the river with the boys being way ahead of me racing each other, I saw a lovely picture playing out in front of me. A Momma was on her raft with a little boy, maybe 18 months old, in her lap. He had the look of a Downs Syndrome baby. He was trying to lap up the water. Momma was ever so gently stopping him every time. It was an adorable picture. At the time I wondered at this significance but gave God thanks for it anyway.

When it came this lady's turn for getting out of the pool, she was ahead of me. I had just gotten to the area as she was stepping out. The water was maybe two and a half feet where she was and over four feet out where I was.

All of a sudden in my spirit, out loud like someone was standing next to me, I heard, "*Stop, wait for it!*"

Then I saw as in slow motion, the baby slip from his mother's arms down into the water, being sucked down into the undercurrent, out to the river area. I heard again, out loud, *"Wait for it!"* I saw the baby going deeper and deeper under the water, heading straight for me. The frantic mother was fighting, trying to get through the crowd. Then I heard *"Now! Now!"* I dove down into the water, grabbed the baby and came up.

He blew out bubbles, sputtered and squirmed in my arms. He was okay! The mother came running in the water as fast as she could towards us. I popped that baby on my other hip with a strong grip on him, held out my hand and said, "Calm down!" She was visibly crying, "I'm not mad at him! I couldn't get all those x'!*# people to move!" I handed her baby back to her and he immediately tried to wiggle out of her arms. She exited the pool quickly, baby in her arms, and said not one word of thanks to me. It's okay. The safe baby was thanks enough for me.

WALKING WITH JESUS

In early 1996 I had a dream I was walking with Jesus in the Sinai Desert. I could feel the warm sand beneath my feet and hot dry air all around me.

I was crying. I told Jesus how I had loved Him all my life. The circumstances of an abusive marriage and now being alone seemed so unfair. Couldn't He please send me a good husband to help me and my sons?

Jesus listened to all my cares and concerns. Then He held up His hand. He said simply, "I will send you someone to walk your path with you."

That was the year Mark Peyron became born again in the Holy Spirit. He sang in tongues for over 45 minutes. That was when he turned his heart to God.

We met in November of 1997.

In 1996 Mark went to a family reunion. Their picture was in the local paper. They named Mark with his wife, Debbie. At the time no one was with him and he had no girlfriend much less a wife.

The year before he met me he dreamed of going bowling with a family he had never seen before. It was me and the boys.

We married on August 7, 1999.

I could argue against pre-destiny, but I think I know too much. Or just maybe, it's choices. Choices set before us. Like when Jesus said, "Choose life and have it to the full."

What a wonderful idea!

What if everybody chose life to the full?

THE WAY

In 1998, Mark and I were at Holy Thursday Mass at St. Michael's. We were engaged at the time. The boys were spending Easter week with Clarence. After mass, Mark came back to my apartment and stayed with me. I got up at 4 am to eat a snack. I was hungry. A poem started to appear in my head.

The first line went through, I thought, "Gee, that was interesting." The second line went through my head and I stopped eating. In the middle of the third line, I grabbed second grade paper and a broken pencil. I wrote as hard and as fast as I could. At one point I couldn't keep up so I cried out, "Please! I lost that last line! Please back up and give it to me again!"

It did.

When I finished all 32 lines, I went upstairs and woke Mark. I read to him the Easter Story the Lord had given me. What a blessing!

You see, I am not a poet the way I am not a writer, until God comes in the picture. Then, I am everything He called me to be.

What about you?

"THE WAY"

It was the night before Easter and all through the house,
Not a creature was stirring, not even a mouse.
The prisoners were hung on their trees as onlookers cried,
In hopes that our Lord would come down, if only He tried.
There we stood at His feet, so despondent, so despaired,
As our Lord bowed His head, the ground shook,
The veil in the temple teared.
We took Him down and buried Him in a fresh hewn cave,
That Joseph of Arimethea thought he might save.
And on the third day there arose such a clatter,
We arose from our room to see what was the matter.
It was the women of our group, shouting in the street,
"Come in", we cried, "so we can all meet."
Magdalene said with tears in her eyes,
"He said He would. He said He would rise!"
I said, "Hold on, wait a minute. Tell this story true.
What on this earth has happened to you?"
"We went to His tomb to anoint Him with oil.
We worried on how we'd move the rock,
on this we did toil.
But when we got there, the rock was all cleared.
We thought this was strange when a young man appeared.
He said to us, "Why dost thou look for the living among
the dead?
Look there, up the road ahead."
A man was walking, to him I did cry,
"Sir, did you see any passers by?"
And He said, "Mary, it is I."
After His forty days so did He ascend,
To His Glory, His Kingdom, till the Earth comes to an end.
What is the meaning of this story do you say?
That Jesus lived and died for us to show us The Way.

Jesus said unto her, "I am the resurrection, and the life: he that believeth in me, though he were dead, yet shall he live: And whosoever liveth and believeth in me shall never die. Believeth thou this?
John 11:25-26

Believeth thou this?

WARNING!

When Mark and I were first married, maybe not quite two years, all the boys were living with us. We were a lively household. I worked part time so I could be home when the kids got off the bus after school.

One day I came in shortly after the guys got home. Ben had given a ride to someone he met at the local coffee shop. I came through the living room and saw this man in the kitchen. Up until then, anyone our children had brought over as friends we treated as family. Hello! How are ya! Nice to meet you. Are you hungry?

Not this time. This boy looked at me, and I stopped. He was dark, and I don't mean his color. There was black all around him. I said to my son, "Ben, honey, can I see you in the back bedroom?"

He said, "Sure Momma."

I stayed very calm.

"Son, you have to get this man out of our house. Lose him. Make sure he can never find his way back here again. I've never told you that you can't have a friend, but not this one, son." He nodded his head yes, walked into the kitchen and said, "Come on, we have to leave."

About five years later, this man went on a killing spree. He killed several family members while robbing them. He is in prison for life.

When God sends you messages, inclinations, warnings, heed them.

It may well save your life.

A CHRISTMAS MIRACLE

In the beginning of our third year of marriage, Mark and I had several people, who were not acquainted with each other, come forward to tell us that we were to go look for land, build a home and even who our builder would be. Since we do not believe in coincidence, we started early in the new year of 2002 looking for land. I wrote on a piece of paper "$18,000.00" and "for sale by owner." That was how we would know the land when we saw it. Mark even got the feeling of where we should drive. When we stepped onto the land, the Holy Spirit fell on me from my feet up. That's it. We were home.

We did indeed buy the land for $18,000. Everything went well and we were in before Christmas. We had many bible studies and prayer groups in that home.

By the fourth year of our marriage, and two years into our new home, my back broke, it fractured at LL5, S1. We had no health insurance. The muscles along the left sciatic nerve, from the gluteus medius to the Achilles tendon, froze. It was like a charley horse 24 hours/seven days a week. All the doctors could do was put me down with medication. From the pain, my temperature would go up to 100 degrees and my hair fell out in clumps. My blood pressure rose week after week.

After seven weeks of incredible pain, I laid on the floor at 3 am during Thanksgiving week, and cried out to the Lord, "I know you are God. You can do anything! Take me up! Get me out of here! Take me home! I don't want to be here anymore! You can do it! I don't want to be a wife or a mother!" My husband was on the floor next to me rebuking every word out of my mouth. Our youngest son, Andy, was hollering in the hallway, "Momma, stop it! You are scaring me!"

I heard a voice as if someone was standing next to me, I believe an angel said, *"Hang on! Your Christmas Miracle is coming! Your Christmas Miracle is coming!"* Being in the frame of mind I was in, I cried out again, "Christmas! It's not even Thanksgiving!" With my next breath, I said, "But not my will, but thine be done." My husband rubbed anointed oil on my back and leg and prayed over me for two hours. I was finally able to get back into bed and slept a little while until my next round of medicine was due.

While this was going on, I played praise music over and over again until I wore out a CD. The doctor scheduled me for an epidural block. It was Christmas time, and my husband Mark was a bench jeweler. He was pressed for time and had no time to stay and help me afterwards. He took me over to the hospital that morning and the nurses prepared me for the procedure. The head nurse in charge of me blew the right vein three times trying to put in an IV for medication distribution.

When they finally got me ready and wheeled me back to the operating room, the anesthesiologist ran the medication for the block down the wrong leg two times! By this time, I had bilateral inflammation and pain on both sides!

Mark brought me home, and my good friend Margaret stayed with me and cooked us a lovely beef stew as she waited for the next round of people who came to help. My cousins came and brought us dinner. By that time I was in terrible pain. I was breaking out in a cold sweat, and started to moan and yell. Gail told me as she was leaving our home, "Deb, you aren't praying hard enough! I'll be praying for you."

The next day my dear friend Mary came and stayed the whole weekend with us. She cooked meals and did dishes, made cookies, and brought me wholesome treats.

Anything that might cheer me up, she did. We prayed together and cried together. She took wonderful care of me. Mark owes a debt here he can't repay. It took all the stress off of him.

The day Mary had to go back home, our friends Lee and Anne called. They wanted to come and see us the next evening. It was soon to be their 25th wedding anniversary, and they wanted Mark to make Anne an opal ring for her present. It would be very nice to see them.

The next morning while praise music was playing, I was laying on the floor trying to wrap a few Christmas gifts for our children. All of a sudden I heard beside me, *"be very sorry for everything you have ever done."*
I took off my glasses, put my head on the floor and cried for half an hour before the Lord. I had a repentant heart. I did not understand that I was being prepared for what was to come.

When the Schwarz's came over that evening, I was laying back in the recliner sweating with pain. Anne conducted her business with Mark quickly. She came over and sat on the couch by her husband, took a good look at me and said, "Debbie, you look terrible."

I replied, "I know Anne, but I keep hearing somebody next to me saying over and over that my Christmas miracle is coming. I believe I am going to have a miracle sometime this season!"

Anne got really excited and grabbed Lee by his arm. She said to him, "Lee, did you hear that? Debbie is going to get a Christmas miracle! We believe in that too!" Then she looked at me and said, "Lee's hands are anointed like the Apostles."

I knew right then and there my time for full healing had come. Lee and Anne looked at each other. She said, "You have to ask him in faith." I asked Lee, "Would you please allow the Holy Spirit to enter you and heal me?" He said, "Why sure!" as if I had asked him to go get me a glass of milk.

Mark and Lee gently laid me on the floor. All I could see were knees. Mark was on his knees at my feet, Anne sitting on the couch beside us, and Lee on his knees at the middle of my back. He said to me, "Debbie, say a prayer in your head. I will know when to start." In my head I said, "Lord, I come before you humbly. Please find nothing in me that would cause you to turn away." He put one hand on my head and the other hand started down my back without touching me. He was inches above me. Immediately I felt heat. It felt hotter and hotter, until he got to the place that was damaged. I was yelling, "Hot! Hot!" Anne was giggling on the couch. She knew what was coming!

Then the damaged disc area began to tingle, to incite as if it were waking up from a sleep. The nerves were firing up! The left lateral muscle LL5/S1 moved back in place. I *felt* the disc heal, wiggle and move back into place. Lastly, the right lateral muscle moved into place as well. At that point, Lee put his hand on my back and it felt like a "surgeon closing from surgery". All the pain ended. Gone.

Lee sat back. In an instant I jumped up all by myself! I could've flew! I yelled, "Yyyyyiiiipppiieee!" Then I started to cry.

We all started to cry. Mark cried out, "Praise the Lord!" It was an instantaneous miracle.

I looked up at Lee and asked, "How can this be?"

And all of a sudden it felt like 2,000 years ago as he replied, "Woman, your faith has saved you."

I asked him again, "What did it feel like when the Holy Spirit entered you and healed me?"

He said he felt tremendous joy. He told me that I

had no stoppers and that my faith was complete.

Now, I could stand again and sit. We laughed and cried. Like Peter's mother-in-law after she was healed by Jesus, I got up and served people drinks and snacks. It was the least I could do. The fracture was healed and I knew my sins were forgiven. What a glorious day.

I couldn't speak a whole sentence for three days. I was overwhelmed. My muscles were tired due to the stress of what they had been through, and I did physical therapy in my home with a book we found on line as my guide. The next day I could dress and drive myself once again. I could walk by myself.

Three weeks after my healing, I was laying on the family room floor doing my daily physical therapy, and I was cold. There was a draft coming in from the patio doors. From my side view, I saw a man in white pick up my blanket off the couch and bring it over and lay it on top of me. I said, 'Thank you." No one replied because no one was there. I went down the hall. Andy was in his room doing homework, and Mark was in our bedroom working on book work.

I tell you, it was an angel sent to comfort me after all I had been through.

God, being no respecter of persons, if He will do this for me, what will He do for you? Evidently, all we have to do is ask, and receive.

WALNUTS

Joan had friends named Joyce and Jim. Jim became very ill. Subsequently, they told Joan about it. Jim had a brain tumor. They asked Joan to pray over him. She complied. Joan prayed a very simple prayer, that the brain tumor would dry up and die. It would look like a dead walnut.

Well, each day Jim felt a little better and a little better. He went back to his doctor on his scheduled visit, and they took an x-ray.

The doctor came out and said, "This cancer has dried up like a walnut!"

The cancer died and Jim didn't.

That's what happens when believer's tell the problem specifically what to do in Jesus' name. And it did and in short order!

This is just like Jesus. He cursed the fig tree for having no fruit and it dried up.

God likes everything and everyone to be fruitful. Fruit on a tree or in a person. We should always be about planting seeds where ever they will grow!

After all, God loves orchards. They were all over the Garden of Eden!

MINDLESS HELP

My husband, Mark, was a bench jeweler. That means he was a craftsman. He could build, repair, or clean anything in the art of jewelry. His busiest season was from mid-November to December 24th. From Thanksgiving to Christmas Eve. I probably got to see him two whole days. I called myself the "Christmas Widow". He hated it when I would say that!

Christmas Day was shared with many a family and friends. But, December 26th is our day! We ask for the same gifts every year, cash or tickets to the movies or restaurant cards to eat out on. That way we get a whole day to play, shop, eat and go see movies all on other peoples' nickels. It's a wonderful treat, and we have a blast together.

Mark had always said I don't pay enough attention to my surroundings. December 26th, 2006 was nothing unusual for me. We had just finished lunch at a nice restaurant in the shopping mall. I was walking and talking away as we walked toward the curb to go to the car. All of a sudden without missing a beat in the conversation, I left my husband's side, and walked over to a van at the side of the curb.

There was a little girl trying to close a big van door. Inside the van was the mother at the steering wheel, two other little children strapped into their seats, and an elderly grandmother sitting in her seat by the door, trying to help her close it from her seat. Again, I was in full conversation with my husband. I took a break to say, "I got this." I picked the little girl up and put her in the front seat, closed her door, and then closed the big van door for the family.

I remember hearing "Thank you! Thank you!"

Saints, I tell you, I did not know what I had done until I closed the second door!

I went back over to my husband's side still "jawing" away. He looked at me intently.

I stopped and said, "What?"

He replied with a smile, "How did you know they needed help?"

I replied, "I didn't know. I didn't see them until I was over helping them."

By this time, he was smiling even bigger, "That's my little helper angel."

Isn't it interesting that my natural eyes were closed but my spiritual eyes were open, and available for God to use.

Halleluiah!

My prayer for you?
Be open, too.

GOD SPEAKS

In the summer of 2007, I was on my way to work in New Albany. I cried because the business I had tried so hard to build to help people, was being torn down by new owners fighting, and I had no say so. I knew my days there were numbered. I wasn't paid for almost a year, and I finally left eight months later.

I was crying out to God. Then, on that clear morning, I heard out loud, rolling thunder and out of it came the voice of God saying, *"I HAVE HEARD YOUR CRY. KNOW HOW MUCH I LOVE YOU."*

Instantly, complete joy came over me! I laughed with tears running down my face! This is the only time I have heard my Abba's voice so far.

FEEDING THE POOR

The reason I called this an every day miracle was because this should be an every day miracle in someone's life. It just happened to be mine and his.

I was having a busy day with lots of housework and errands to do. In between breaths I called out, "Order my steps, Lord!"

On the way to run errands, I again said, "Lord, allow me to touch a life today in a positive way! Thanks!" I went to the grocery and the shoe store. My last errand was to the local grocery store to pick up a pair of sun glasses. It was a very hot day during the record breaking summer of 2010. I finished up and headed out the door wondering why God didn't send someone for me to give a kind word or to pray over. I walked out of the store in a hurry.

A young man was sitting on the bench outside the doorway and mumbled something to me as I walked past. I hardly noticed him. I stopped. Confused, I walked back to him. His head was bowed, his shoulders hunched down as if in despair. I said, "I'm sorry. I didn't hear you. What did you say?"

He looked up at me. His face was beet red and he was sweating. He stammered, "Could you spare some change?" He looked as if he had been out in the heat for a long time. The sum total I had on me was 38 cents. I told him, "I'm so sorry. All I have is 38 cents." He hung his head down.

I started to walk away. I heard very clearly and loud in my spirit, ***"Ask him when is the last time he has eaten."*** I turned back around and spoke to him again, "Young man, when was the last time you ate?"

He responded with a small amount of hope in his voice, "A nice person bought me a drink!" He pointed to it by his feet. "I was so thirsty", he declared.

Again I said, "When was the last time you had anything to eat?"

He put his head down again, "Yesterday."

As the mother of three sons that statement about broke me. I knew all we had was $15.00 in the bank but that child was getting a meal! "Get up boy!", I cried. "Get out of this heat! We are going into the sandwich shop and get you some lunch!" I wasn't asking him, I was telling him! He obediently followed me inside the store.

I bought him the biggest sandwich, biggest drink, chips and dessert they had! I listened to his story, informed him that the local police department may be able to help him get a ticket back home to his mother. Then I prayed for him.

The next time I went to the grocery, he was not there. In my heart, I believe he got to go home.

Stay safe, young man.

If it was in your power to keep someone from going hungry, wouldn't you help too?

I knew you would.

So does God.

VISIONARY

This happened in the fall of 2007. We were having friends over for dinner. I walked to the back bedroom to call the boys for dinner. I was standing in their doorway when I felt the house jolt. Hard! It was as if something had just slammed into the earth! Not an earthquake, but a moving of the whole planet! I screamed. At this point, I did not realize I was seeing in the Spirit and not in the flesh. Within two seconds everything in my sight turned upside down, the whole room and everything. I saw Mark and Andy fall off their beds and onto the floor. I saw their beds fall down on top of them. I screamed again and bent to my knees onto the floor, not knowing which way was up. I screamed again, "Did you feel that? Did you see that?"

The boys were scared then. Andy cried out, "What's wrong, Momma!"

I said again, "Didn't you feel that? The earth moved!" I knew something was coming!

I worried over this. I wondered if this was prophesy for the year 2012, or whether this was a personal prophesy for me. During that time we did have a tremendous upheaval in our lives with the loss of my job and the financial stress it put us under.

That spring, Mark and I went to Mary's Farm in Southern Indiana. There was a priest there who was a visionary. I told him my experience. He said it was God's way of warning us about what was going to happen. He said God knew it would turn my world upside down.

JESUS

So many of the things I have experienced come out of ordinary events. I may not get a full interpretation for months or years.

In the spring of 2009 Mark and I were still renting a house, waiting on God's help to turn things around for us.

One night, our friend Kelly had come to spend the night with us. After dinner we were all sitting around in the living room talking. I must have mentioned feeling a little achy. Kelly is a massage therapist and a good prayer warrior. She volunteered to use gentle touch and prayer on my knees and elbows and where she was directed in her heart to pray over.

She stood me up in the middle of the living room and started praying for my health and wisdom. Then she sat me down on the couch and went to pray a second time over my knees, elbows, and my heart. When she got to my heart area she cried out! I immediately went into a vision. It lasted several seconds.

I looked all around me and I was no longer on my living room couch. I was in a crowd of people, dressed as they were 2,000 years ago. We were standing on a dusty dirt road. We were in a town square with earthen and sand block buildings around us. In the middle of this area was a man hunched down writing something in the dirt. He was explaining a parable, teaching the crowd. He had on what looked to be a white woolen robe tied at the waist. I could see the dirt and dust at the bottom of his hem. I could see his sandals. He had long dark hair and a beard. When he looked up, I knew it was Jesus, Yeshua of Nazareth. He pointed to a man in the crowd and motioned him over. Jesus was calling him to join him. The man looked from right to left, then back at Jesus, and pointed to himself,
"Me?"

Jesus nodded. He stepped forward. Then I was back.

I could see normally again. Natural sound came back. Kelly and I both hollered! Mark was impatiently waiting for an explanation of what all the commotion was about! "I've seen a vision!" I cried out.

Kelly said, "Debbie, I went to touch your heart and Jesus was there!" She had seen something too.

I told them what I had seen. She thought it meant I was an apostle of Jesus in another lifetime. I said, "I don't think so. I think it means He is in my heart, and He is calling me to be an apostle now! I am to listen to His teachings and do what He tells me."

Kelly went on to say, "He is calling you to do something big!"

I am only now, a year out from this, following what He has been trying to tell me all this time. Write His book. Be obedient. Be an example. Be an apostle.

Okay.

FRED

Our Pastor has been born again and called to preach for over 33 years as of the year 2010. He was a professional musician, playing along side him was his wife, Jeanne and his best friend, Bill Mauck.

Shortly after he was born again in the winter of 1977, he got to meet Jesus.

One evening Fred was in his kitchen in a little town in Illinois. He turned around and there stood Jesus in his kitchen. He saw Jesus in the flesh, very real and tangible.

Then Jesus spoke to Fred, "Let go." Fred replied, "I can't. I'm afraid. What if I get hurt?" Jesus explained to him, "I have put angels in front of you lest you dash your foot upon the ground. Let go, Fred. Let go."

Fred thought for a moment and then he said, "Alright. I will. I'll let go." Jesus then told him he was having a heart attack but he would be okay now. He would stay here for now.

At the last word from Jesus' mouth, angels led Fred down as he fell from the sky. He went into what he thought was a cool, dry valley. That was when he fell into his own mouth, into his own body. His body felt very heavy. He wanted to stay out and go with Jesus, but it was not his time.

Because Jesus conquered death, Pastor Fred beat death many times in his life.

And God is no respecter of persons, what He does for one, He will do for another.

Even you!

THROUGH BEN'S EYES
BY PAUL BENJAMIN EARL MERK

We are the dreams of a never-sleeping God, a patchwork of hopes, joys, nightmares and fears. Our world sprang forth as his longing for companionship unfolded in the restless dreaming of his slumbering subconscious.

God is the living spirit. His presence is felt in the core of all living things. From the greatest peaks of life to the lowest piece of grass which grows in the light, the power of God is present. All things which exist God exists within. My spirit is but a drop of that infinite and intangible ocean which is God. My body and all bodies are his desires made flesh and all life is his hopes made good.

In the spirit of the world we are made in his image. Life begets unto life. For as God creates so must we. And as God has created and followed his own dream so must we. As every flower which gives its pollen to breed new life is working to do the will of God, so are we all.

God is embodied by a careful love which is tempered with the full range of emotions. When the storms clap loudly, God's awesome rage is felt most purely, although the storm may be the very cause of the spring flowers. God resides within the seasons and his ageless face can be seen painted across the rocks and deserts and flora and fauna of his vast and ever changing world.

He takes loving care in tending to the details which have allowed life to exist. He is an artist and a chemist, we are his living canvas. He breathes life across the borders and shades the background until pure. As living works of art God gives us the opportunity to paint ourselves. Who we are is a product of where we were; and all that together with God's will creates who we will become.

Our understanding of God has grown as time has moved onward. All life springs forth from God and all life is inseparable from God. Like raindrops we fall as spirits made flesh. All we think, feel, and experience shall be returned to God. God makes us more full, more whole, and we fulfill the purpose of God's desire for us to know Him in all His many facets. Again I say, all life flows forth from God and all life shall be returned unto God.

The value and purpose of knowing subjective good and evil are as a mirror for one another. For how do we know what passion is without its lesser? And is a passion's opposite its lesser or is it an unrivaled equal. For in the heart of God there are a million shades of color, but without the furthest reaches of a spectrum could the in between be known?

God is passionate and resides within the deepest part of our hearts. When drawn to create with words, or music, or art, or love, then the heart of God is expressed in our works. When we follow our passions, and not the petty worries which life presents, then God smiles upon our faces. His light shines out and touches our souls and for a moment, when following passions, our souls can touch upon the infinite.

Miraculous Interventions™ II

Modern Day Priests, Prophets, Pastors & Everyday Visionaries

By
Deborah Aubrey-Peyron

Miraculous Interventions™ II
Modern Day Priests, Prophets, Pastors & Everyday Visionaries
By Deborah Aubrey-Peyron

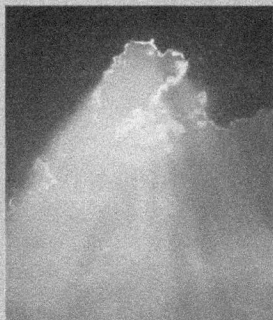

"What I tell you in the dark, speak in the daylight."
Matthew 10:27, NIV

"Call to me and I will answer thee, and shew thee great and mighty things, which thou knowest not."
Jeremiah 33:3 KJ

Amazing stories from various pastors, lay ministers and those who are called to walk in the office of the miraculous - their experiences with the Lord and the divine intervention they have witnessed.

MEDJUGORJE
Father Bernie Weber

Father Bernie stated he was in Medjugorje in 1987, a place he really didn't want to go to. This is his story of how God got him there.

In 1987, while at a local parish, Father Bernie was being "pestered" by a couple who had just come back from the Medjugorje shrine. They thought he should make a pilgrimage to Yugoslavia. It was not in his heart to go. But, after a time, he told them he would go back to the rectory and pray before a big creosote cross. (An 8 x 8 railroad tie size cross). He "put out a fleece". He said, "If I stand in front of the cross and the moon is on the other side of the cross, that's a sign from God and I'll go to Medjugorje."

Well, the moon was behind his back and he was facing the cross. He said to himself, "Good, I don't have to go to Medjugorje." As he was walking back to his rectory the Lord spoke to him. The Lord God said, "THAT'S NO SIGN. WRITE YOUR PROVINCIAL." This took him by surprise. But in obedience he wrote a letter that was not very encouraging. In fact, it was a pretty neutral letter. He expected to get a letter back saying something like, "It's not approved by the church, it's nonsense, etc." Father Bernie did not want to go to Yugoslavia. He reasoned, "The Blessed Mother is right here. Why should I have to go all the way over there?"

The provincial wrote back. He not only allowed Father Bernie to go but encouraged him to go! Father Bernie's reply was? "Aaaaahhhh!!" But what could he say? So he went.

While there, he met a couple who agreed with his ministry of healing. They started sending him people to be prayed over. *Everyone* they sent to him was healed!

Now the church had not yet given its official approval. One of the laymen involved with Our Lady of Fatima was there. He was a Fatima Crusader, and they were adamantly opposed to Medjugorje because the pope had yet to consecrate it with the Bishops of Russia. And in their eyes, every disaster that was happening in the land was because this hadn't been consecrated yet.

This man and his wife came to see Father Bernie at 10:30 in the evening. They came to where Bernie was staying. He said to him, "Father Bernie, there is an Irish lady with bad knees. She has had to cancel all her visitations to the Marian shrine because she can't walk to them. Would you go over and please pray for her?"

"Alright."

Father Bernie went over to where she was staying. There was a courtyard there with a lot of people in it. It just so happened they met a Croatian man who lived in the United States. He spoke perfect English and perfect Croatian. The couple invited him to come along with them. Father Bernie prayed over the Irish lady. Her knees were healed in front of the Fatima Crusader and the Croatian man. Now, she could continue making her visitation to the Marian Center.

There was another man there, an Englishman. He also had bad knees. Father Bernie asked him if he needed prayer. The Englishman replied very stoically, "No, that's alright Father. You have more important things to do."

"Okay."

While Father was still making this pilgrimage, there was a set of grandparents living at the house where he was staying. They had a son who was married and had a little three year old girl. The grandmother asked through a translator, "Would you pray over my three year old granddaughter? She has never walked in her life." That was all they told him.

"Sure."

It was quite cool out and the little child had on several layers of clothing. The mother was holding her. They were all outside gathered around, the mother, father, the grandparents, Father Bernie, the interpreter and the little girl.

Father Bernie put his hand on the little girl's hair but she didn't like that. He then put his hand on her back. While they were praying he felt heat coming out of her back, through all the layers of clothing and into his hand! When they got through praying, through the translator, Father told the little girl's mother to squat down with her. He told the father to do the same. He was a little distance from his wife and daughter. Then, he told the father, to call his daughter.

The mother let go of the child and she waddled all on her own to the father. They all started crying. They all went into praising God. Everyone started shouting, "It's a miracle! It's a miracle!" Later on, the little girl was standing all by herself playing with the hair on her head. The grandmother started yelling in Croatian. The translator translated the grandmother's outburst. "Look! She could never do that before!" She had never even stood on her own.

Afterwards, Father Bernie found out the reason she had never walked before. At six months old, she had spinal meningitis. It ate away the myelin film around the spinal cord. All the electrical signals got shorted out going down the branch to the legs. The signals never got to the legs so she couldn't walk. She couldn't stand at all for three years before that day. Father Bernie continued his story, "When I felt heat go down her back that was God healing the myelin so fast that heat came out. And that's why she could walk now. Within five minutes, she was running."

This was a level four miracle.

THE HAND OF GOD
Lee & Anne Schwarz

This story is taken straight from the e-mail Lee sent me while we were corresponding about this book. As I wrote his stories about miracles, a series of them unfolded right before our very eyes. This all took place over the span of ten days. Sometimes in life, events happen as if all intertwined by a beautiful golden thread. As if the hand of God was and is still moving across the waters. Lee wrote:

We have more stories about God's Intervention than you know about. And they happened in the last week. As you know, Anne was scheduled for surgery July 12th to replace her terrible right knee. The surgery coordinator from the hospital called last week and said, "And you will be one of the very first patients in the new hospital wing." Tilt. Did she mean as in new carpets and new everything? A sniff test was in order. So, last Friday we went to the hospital for a sniff test. Sure enough, it was $500M, 12 floors of new carpet and plastic. It wasn't too bad as we walked into the wing. It was not too bad on the 10th (orthopedic) floor with all the empty rooms. Then, down the hall to the other end where there were a couple of rooms with a couple of beds in them, WHAM! Like a heart attack it hit Anne: her lungs were on fire, the chest pain was intense, her lungs were shutting down. The ER was not an option since it was in the same building.

Anne escaped the building, got to the car and took an Advair puff. She quickly returned to normal. We placed an emergency call to her pulmonologist who saw her on Monday.

Anne's doctor listened to her lungs. She said, "Surgery is off. There is no way we can keep you alive for the three days. You'll need to be in the hospital, and there is no place else you can get on the schedule this summer and be back in the classroom by September. By the way, where do you live?" Anne told her. The doctor replied, "Living there, you are constantly at a subclinical level of poisoning. That is why you react to everything else much too strongly. You have to move."

Move instead of surgery.

Ri-i-ight.

Well, at God's insistence we had agreed to rent a house a month ago and put our home on the internet. Within 24 hours we had a call on the home, but the rental deal fell through. So, we took our home off the internet. Last Sunday, the same woman who had called about the place a month ago, called asking if it was still for sale. Conditionally, yes. We visited awhile over the phone and she told me her family had recently put her father in a nursing home and had to sell his house.

"Oh? Where?"

"Snohomish." (Our target city)

We asked for the address and what the home was like. So, it went like this.

Friday: Emergency

Sunday: House talk.

Monday: Told we must move.

Tuesday: Looked at the house.

Wednesday: Met with the realtor at the house.

Thursday: Accepted our offer at 20% below the asking price.

Friday: Loan application finished.

Saturday: Met with the inspector.

While I was at the bank needing to know how to make out the earnest money check, the realtor called me. While I was talking with the realtor who needed to know the time frame for the inspection, the inspector called me with the answers to the realtor's questions!

Now, we still need to sell this place, but after all the above, do we trust God for the outcome? You bet! A couple of months ago, as we were all in a dither about moving or not moving and the surgery, I was in prayer about it all.

God said to me then, "I HAVE THE ANSWER. I *AM* THE ANSWER."

Ya think?
Blessings,

Lee

RESURRECTION OF THE DEAD
Pastor Ivie Dennis

Pastor Ivie Dennis and the worship team found themselves on the fourth day at ten in the morning, in a small remote village. They walked through the area passing out tracts and witnessing to anyone who would listen.

Suddenly, a woman came bolting out of her hut door screaming! The interpreter told them the baby in her arms was not breathing. The ten people on the team ran to her! The six week old infant was indeed blue and non-responsive.

The team members prayed in spirit and in tongues. They laid hands on the baby. They commanded the spirit of death to come out of that baby! They prophesied, "He will live and not die!"

Before their eyes, the infant boy took a breath, then another and another until his color was fully back, and he was responsive with a loud cry!

Everyone cried and they prophesied a great call over his life!

God showed up that day large and in charge and gave that baby his life back. They were sure he was rescued to be a mighty warrior.

The village people and the whole group saw an instant miracle. As they left the village, the word went forth before them just like the apostles of old.

SHOE BOXES
Pastor Ivie Dennis

It was Christmas time, December of 2004. The Board of Lifeline Outreach Ministry decided to have a shoe box ministry for the poor children in the area. They had applied back in the fall for a grant from a large corporation. They hoped it would have been there before then, but as December rolled on, the money had not yet made its appearance.

The group looked to their bank account to buy hats, gloves, crayons, socks, pencils and small toys. There were at least 25 children they knew of that would be attending the December 24th Christmas Eve party. There was $140.00 to be spread out among the 25. Pastor Ivie said to wait. "Wait on God." December 20th there was nothing. Prayers went up. December 21st there was still nothing. Rats. I confess that I had a stomach ache over it all!

On December 22nd the dam broke! The angels came through! At 10 am a check for the promised $2,500.00 showed up! Dollar Tree, here they came! I was blessed to be there that day. "All hands on deck!" We wrapped packages as fast as we could!

Then there was another knock on the door. A local company donated a whole host of turkeys! Wow!! Cooks! Man your stations! LOM served 500 hot meals on Christmas Eve. We gave out 25 presents to the children of the area. The boxes were stuffed to the gills!

One of the recipients was an 18 year old young man. He stood there crying, holding the box tight in his hands. "Why are you crying?" we asked. He told us it was his only Christmas present.

God gave to LOM beyond our wildest dreams! This is what happens when the love of Jesus impacts humanity.

NOTRE DAME
Pastor Jim and Ann Carter

By the early to mid-1970's, the Catholic Charismatic community at Notre Dame was holding conferences of the Holy Spirit. One of them was led by "The Fabulous Five". These were five protestant ministers who walked in the power of the Holy Spirit. Their mission was to teach Catholic clergy and lay people about being born again, or Charismatic's - same gifts with different names. Pastor Jim and Ann Carter, some other pastors, and their entire group went up to Notre Dame in South Bend, Indiana in a big, chartered bus.

Along the way back from South Bend, they were approached by 70 nuns also on the way back from the Notre Dame conference. The nuns asked them how they could be saved, too! They wanted to be baptized in the Holy Spirit.

From South Bend to Indianapolis, they all traveled together. And one by one, the nuns were all baptized in the Holy Spirit. The Spirit was prevalent on the bus with them. The ministers preached what God did for us when he raised Jesus from the dead!

When Jesus died and rose, the veil was torn. We as Christians, as brothers in Christ Jesus, can now boldly come before the throne of God.

Every nun received her own prayer language*.

* *This is the gift of "Speaking in Tongues" as in Acts 2:3-4, "And there appeared unto them cloven tongues like as of fire, and it sat upon each of them. And they were all filled with the Holy Ghost, and began to speak with other tongues, as the Spirit gave them utterance."*

BELIEVING ABOVE ALL ELSE
Pastor Jim and Ann Carter

In the 1970's, while Jim and Ann were just getting into their stride with prayer and miracles, they were at a church gathering with about 30 other people. It was for praise and worship, then a meal together.

Well, one of the families present at the meeting had a small child who went to reach up on the table for some food. The problem was it was a very hot dish. And she knocked it over onto herself before anyone could stop her.

In an instant the little girl was scalded with second degree burns over most portions of her body. It all seemed to happen at once. The baby was screaming, everyone was screaming! But the Holy Spirit was with them. The parents grabbed the toddler up, and everyone surrounded them with strong prayers of healing.

Within a few minutes the child calmed down, the blisters went down, and the red skin faded to pink. Then she wiggled out of her Mother's arms and went back to playing.

I love the stories that end with "and they all lived happily ever after."
Bless God.

A FLORIDA CRACKER
Larry and Marilynn Crosier

Shortly after Larry was born again in the Holy Spirit, he started praying for a wife. He wanted a wife with the same heart for Jesus that he had. At 24 years old he started praying and praying. Larry prayed for a year and a half. He even enlisted help! A sweet, elderly lady at his church made it her mission to pray and listen for God's help with this matter too. I should note here that Larry has always lived in Southern Indiana.

Almost a year and a half later, a very nice young lady from Florida had just started praying for God to send her a husband. Well, unknown to the both of them, they each had mutual friends who knew them both. God spoke to these friends, "**Put these two together**".

Larry wrote Marilynn a five page letter only knowing her name and that she was a Christian. He poured his heart out.

When Marilynn received his letter after only a few days of asking God for a husband, she had to pause to reply to this letter. This was important. She knew this would mean the difference in the rest of her life. It took Marilynn three weeks to put together everything she wanted to tell him too. When Larry received the letter he knew it was from his future wife. As soon as his eyes could finish reading the words on the pages, he called her and they talked for over two hours. Yes indeed, this surely had to be a God intervention. They wrote back and forth, sent tapes and went to meet each other's families. Within seven short months, they trusted God and each other and wed May 15th, 1982. They trusted God then to put them together, and they trust God now.

But this is just the beginning of their journey together.

MOVE
Larry and Marilynn Crosier

One day, in Marilynn's heart and mind, she felt God speak to her to move. He wanted them to sell their house, quit their jobs and move.

She did not question Him when this word came down.

All she said was, "When, Lord?"

He replied, "**Three and a half months**."

Marilynn asked again, "Where to Lord?"

"Jasper, Indiana."

"Okay Lord but You have to tell Larry."

His reply was, "**I have already told him!**"

That night when Larry came home from work, he too had a word from the Lord confirming what she had been told.

In their minds and hearts, as they sold their first home, they envisioned what their new place would be like, even what it would cost. They put their petitions up to the Lord.

They got everything they wanted. The type of home it was, the land, the stocked fishing pond, even the amount of rent! A very nice Catholic family owned it and just wanted someone good to live there. It seemed God answered both of their prayers together.

The Crosiers told God everything they wanted and He delivered it all to them.

Tell God what you want.
Watch Him deliver it to you, too, in His own time.

COINCIDENCE ON TOP OF COINCIDENCE
Fr. Mike Olsen

I've taught a couple of times over the years at TOPS, "Taking Off Pounds Sensibly". My best friend of 38 + years, Vicki Sampson, had asked me to come and teach a class so that everyone would have all the information they would need to eat healthy the rest of their life.

I could do that.

The day she picked was a day that Mark and I had off together. Wonderful! He could help me giving out papers and fielding questions. In the 10 years of my teaching and being in the wellness field, Mark had never come along to help. But he was happy to do it.

We arrived in Louisville early and spent some quality time with Vicki before class. The regular group showed up that evening along with a new couple, a husband and wife.

Between my talk and questions afterward, the meeting went a little longer than normal. Thankfully, the interest was high, and no one complained. The meeting adjourned shortly after 8:30 pm, and we prepared to leave when I was approached by the new couple.

The man initiated the conversation, "Hello, I'm Father Mike Olsen. You are charismatic." He stated it as if I had been preaching a half hour on the Holy Spirit!

I shook my head, stared at him with confusion planted squarely on my face and said, "How did you know that?" Quite simply he replied, "The Holy Spirit told me."

I responded quickly, "That makes you my brother!"

With a big smile he said, "And that makes you my sister!"

He then introduced his wife to me, and I hollered for Mark to come over and meet these people! "Mark honey! Come quick! The Lord has set up another meeting for us!"

We introduced our spouses. Father Mike went on with the conversation, "The Lord wants us to get together. How can I contact you?"

I gave him one of my business cards with the book Miraculous Interventions on it. He looked at it and said, "Wow. You write books about miracles? We believe in all that too! We see "angel orbs", God's gold and miracles in our church." He smiled.

It didn't take me but a second to say, "We're coming to your church, and I'll write a whole chapter about you all!"

I gave him a copy of my first book, "Miraculous Interventions".

On the way home Mark and I spoke of how amazed we were at how God used the ordinary to bring together the extraordinary and we wondered where this path would lead us.

Fr. Mike Olsen at a gathering May, 2012 in Louisville, KY

HELP A BROTHER OUT
Fr. Mike Olsen

We met this fine couple ten days prior to going on a family vacation to Walt Disney World. Two days after meeting them, I received an e-mail from Father Mike. The Holy Spirit had told him to tell me their whole story in one e-mail.

Mike had lost his job nine months ago. The Olsen's were struggling. They too were going to Florida but not on vacation. Patti's father had died. They had little to no resources to get there.

I printed out their message and laid it on the kitchen table to show to Mark when he got home from work. When he got home and read the e-mail, Mark had the same reaction as me. He said, "I've got $50.00. What have you got?"

I replied, "I've got $50.00 too."

Then Mark said, "What have we got in the way of supplies that we could send with them on the road?"

We went into the back bedroom to check our vacation supplies. There was much more there than the eight of us could use on the whole trip. We set aside an almost full case of bottled waters, boxes of crackers, chips, chocolates and other various snacks to take to our newest set of friends. Evidently they needed us.

A few days later I took their supplies to their home. They were very grateful that two strangers would take their situation to our hearts. After we had chatted a few minutes, Father Mike started a very interesting conversation. He asked me, "Have you ever heard of or seen angelic orbs?"

I had some understanding of what he was talking about and said as much. He asked, "Would you be interested in seeing some pictures of them?"

"You have pictures? Yes! I would love to see them!"

I was all eyes and ears. He had a whole album of them. They were taken with different cameras, different situations and times, various places. It was almost as if they had been with him all of his life.

I asked, "Have you got any objection to being in a book about miracles?"

He laughed and said, "That would be fine!"

We knew our families would see each other again after our trips to Florida.

We wished each other well on our separate journeys, and promised when we came back, we would come to their church to see what it was all about.

At that time, we had no idea of the miraculous journey we were about to embark on. The greatest days, it seemed, were just ahead of us.

JANUARY 1, 2012 - INTRODUCTION
Fr. Mike Olsen

After the best family vacation ever, time seemed to fly by between Halloween and Christmas. The end of 2011 was busier than normal for us. We were used to Mark's hours ramping up to 70 hours a week, but it was our first time to see me have a busy Christmas season as well.

"Christmas Chaos" hit the stores just days before the Thanksgiving weekend. I felt like half the season was already gone! I made many appointments for book signings, school Christmas parties, church teas, radio station interviews and book deliveries to local Kentucky and Indiana book stores.

Our home church shuts down during the holidays so people, including our pastor and his wife could travel to see their families. Every time Mark and I had a free moment, off we flew to the department store for another person that had been inadvertently left off the "good" list.

During this season we did make time to get together for dinner with Larry and Marilynn Crosier. At the end of our evening together, we checked our schedules to see when we could get together again. Our new friendship was off to a very nice start. Larry said, "Deb, the first day I have open is Sunday January 1, 2012."

I replied, "Okay. Hey, do you all want to go with us to the new church over in Louisville? It's the one where the priest is seeing angels and God's gold."

Larry and Marilynn grinned at each other. He said, "That sounds like a plan to me!" I called St. Columba and asked Fr. Mike if that was a good date for us to come by. He said that would be a great date because their Christmas party was to be after the mass. We could stay and fellowship. Wonderful! We agreed to bring a side dish. I called Marilynn to inform her, and all was set.

(See the rest of the story on page 87.)

TOP: Larry and Marilynn Crosier
BOTTOM: Mark, Deborah and Fr Mike Olsen

January 1, 2012 after our first Mass together.

Fr Mike leading the praise and worship before mass on January 1, 2012.

THE MENDING OF MITCH
Mitchell Smith

In all fairness, readers, you need to know that Mitch Smith is my publisher's ex-husband and best friend. But that does not make any of his stories any less interesting!

Mitch is 52 years old as of this writing. I asked him when he thought he came to know the Lord. He had a hard time with that question because he felt he was still coming to know the Lord!

Mitch does not think that miracles are odd. He thinks they happen all the time. In fact, they are so common place we don't even notice them. Except for these following . . .

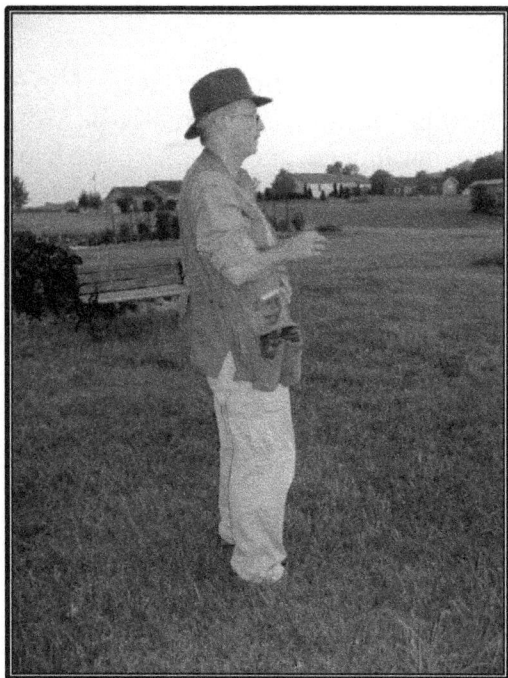

Mitch Smith surveying our land in Indiana 2012

ST. JOSEPH
Mitchell Smith

When Mitch was in the eighth grade, in 1972, he got sick, real sick. He had Glomerulonephritis. He went into Renal Failure, a bad place to be for an eighth grader. Mitch stated back in 1972, compared to today's medicine, all they had was witchcraft!

The doctors could tell he was really sick. At the time they couldn't do much about it. He was in the hospital and not allowed to move around in his bed or get up. He needed kidney dialysis. Mitch was on the schedule to go down and have the procedure when a little old retired nun popped her head in the door. She visited kids who were in dire straights.

She started to talk to him when she realized Mitch was too sick to respond. She said to him, "Don't worry. Saint Joseph is going to take care of his boy."

That night, Mitch told his nurse he needed to go urinate. They brought him the urinal. Normally he would pass an ounce of urine that looked like a dark cola. It was so concentrated and strong it would burn as it passed through.

But this night, he passed close to a liter of normal urine, without dialysis, thank you!

Every half hour to 45 minutes, his body passed normal urine with no pain. He got very little sleep that first night. He weighed 160 pounds with all the held water, and in two days he was back down to the normal weight of a 13 year old boy.

He still has stretch marks from this event.

DADDY
Mitchell Smith

Later in life, Mitch was diagnosed as infertile. He would not be able to be a daddy. It was a horrible diagnosis, and the tests hurt!

While in the Army, Mitch was assigned as a peace keeper for the Camp David Accords in the Sinai Desert. They were stationed in what is now a booming little resort town. But back then it was just another place in the desert. For R & R, (rest and recuperation), the Army sent them to Mt. St. Katrina's Monastery in Mt. Sinai. They were glad to go because even a Monastery was entertaining compared to a spot in the desert!

Mitch spoke with one of the Greek monks. There were no Catholic chaplains for their task force at that time. The monk asked him if he had any children.

Mitch replied, "No."

"Why not?"

"I can't." He went on to explain what the doctors had told him.

Miracle words came forth from the monk's mouth. "I want you to go over to that well and get a drink of water. I am going to go get you a medal."

Mitch went over to the well and did as he was instructed. Then he walked back over to the monk. The monk was giggling.

Mitch's first thought was, "I'm an American. What's wrong with the water?" There were a lot of the men that were suffering with Dysentery.

The monk replied, "We refuse to drink from that well. Any man who drinks from that well will father twins."

"Oh, really?"

Mitch came home on leave. His wife, Mary Dow, did indeed get pregnant. They went for the sonogram and it was twins!

There it was!   Glory!
What a miracle to go from infertile to fathering twins.

Praise Ye the Lord!!

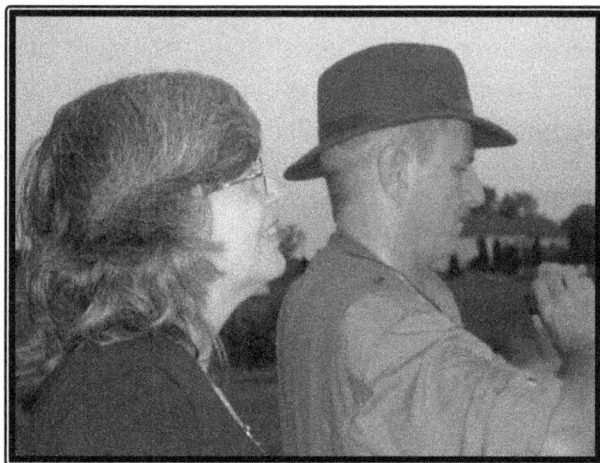

Mitch and Mary Smith (HCAP editor)
observing a beautiful sunset (below) out on
Mark and Deborah's land 2012

SECOND CHANCES
Mitchell Smith

The biggest miracle of Mitch's life is something most people won't recognize as a miracle. In his life he had fallen away from the church and from God. Mitch had trashed his life and the lives of his family. He was marking time, waiting to get old and die. Be done with it. He was actually looking forward to it.

One morning Mitch woke up and he knew he was an absolute mess, yet God loved him unconditionally. Even though Mitch was very far from God, God was still very close to him. He felt God wanted him to get out of bed, get dressed and go to the only church where he knew one was. Mitch was just in time for Sunday service to begin. At the time he woke up, he was not even aware it was Sunday!

Mitch confessed he was a drug user, and it went away. He was healed of it. He was then able to make peace with his family, and they were all for it! It is now an entirely different life for him.

If we compared who Mitch was in 2001 with who he is in 2011, you would not think it to be the same person or the same life at all. I reminded Mitch that God gives second chances.

And my dear brother in Christ reminded me that God gives third, fourth, fifth, sixth, seventh chances, etc...

Laughter erupted from both of us!

MITCH'S TESTIMONY
As Real As Rocks

Mitch is a Roman Catholic. He is amazed constantly at the mercy shown him through things other Catholics take for granted, such as the sacrament of reconciliation, the anointing of the sick and mass on Sunday. He stated, "We don't go there to sing songs or hold hands with each other. Jesus is present in the readings. He is present in the ministers. He is present in the sacrament at the altar. He is present in the congregation. He is there four ways from Sunday."

Mitch went on to say, "When you go to a mass that they are using incense, they are marking another way Christ is present in the mass."

Mitch does not belong to a distant God. He belongs to a Lord who is right with us as He promised. Mitch can go see Him on Sunday. He can be in His presence. I commented, "I believe we can see Him everyday. Jesus walks with us."

He made no comment to this as he went on to say that he can receive Jesus in Communion. And when he strays, he can go to Confession. Any priest can absolve him from his sins because the priest is not acting for himself, he is acting in the persona Christi, the body of Christ, God's hands and feet on this earth.

I again commented, "We are called to be the same." Mitch agreed, "Yes we are! And that is the biggest miracle! That is the one that lets every other miracle in my life happen! We are the body of Christ! The little nun was being Christ for me when she prayed for me. The Greek monk was being Christ for me when he tricked me into drinking the water. For me, it is not a theory or distant, it is as real as rocks!"

SAINT TERESA OF CALCUTTA
Deborah Aubrey-Peyron

PART ONE

The year of the hottest spring and summer on record (2010) in Kentuckiana went into the wettest spring on record **ever**! The mighty Ohio River and all its tributaries overflowed their banks. The even mightier Mississippi River flooded whole towns and regions all the way until it emptied into the Gulf of Mexico.

Gardens had to be replanted over and over again as seeds and saplings drowned in the mix. April saw more tornadoes, over 860 with damage coming out of the west and south that broke records of deadliest and most destructive as well. The season of spring was off to a rough start.

It was the middle of May 2011 when our garden finally took hold. By the end of May, my first book, "Miraculous Interventions." was ready to print the first 200 copies. Why 200 copies? It was all the money this "mom and mom" organization could come up with at the time.

Our dear friend Kelly had also agreed to come on board as illustrator for the new children's book, "Christmas Chaos!" And our landscaping business had taken off like a shot! (I guess no one else wanted to "play in the mud.") We were blessed in all that our hands touched!

Bless God!

Why, even in our sleep we were being blessed - in our dreams, in my dreams.

And it went like this...

I dreamed I was going to meet a visionary. It was not a long journey, but it had its own tribulations associated with the drive. I stopped at a moderate looking brick home. It was a busy place, a work in progress. From children to teenagers and adults, they all had jobs to do. I walked up to the front door, and they ushered me into a small office to wait for her. There was a desk and several chairs sitting around the room. Books lined open faced wooden cabinets along the walls. I did not know the name of this visionary at the time, or what to expect.

She walked into the room still giving orders and recommendations to the people following around after her. She then turned her attention toward me with a big smile.

Her big smile was the only thing big on her! She looked to be about four feet and change tall. And the only way she weighed 100 pounds is if someone put rocks in her pockets!

She started the conversation with great news. She said, "Our Heavenly Mother is very pleased with the book you have written for her Son."

Well, if the dream had stopped right there I'd still be on cloud nine!

But it went on.

How could I explain this to you? The air in the room became "soft", almost palpable with a sweet floral fragrance to it. The visionary was now smiling at someone I couldn't see with my eyes. I was caught up in this heavenly visitation.

She spoke again, "What do you want of us?"

I was stunned to silence. I was being visited by this heavenly host and asked what I would like. They were pleased with my work! I stammered, "Want something? I, I, I want something?" My brain failed me and went to mustard!

Quick! Think!

I was so blessed in the moment I couldn't order my own thoughts!

"Uh, I want all my sons to know Jesus Christ! But I also want a home on our land! No wait!! I want the books to do really well! Then, we can put a home on our land!"

I panicked. I couldn't make up my mind. Could I make a list?

The Visionary looked up to Heaven, shrugged her shoulders with a question on her face. Then she turned to me and said, "I will come back and ask you again."

The scene faded away and I awoke.

I still await her return.

THE KEY
Deborah Aubrey-Peyron

Remember the story about the wettest spring on record? It also ended up being the wettest year on record ever. But in the middle of the downpours, the summer months had all the markings of a drought. First you couldn't plant because the soil was saturated. Then within weeks, it was so dry nothing could grow, unless you knew the key.

Our Mother's Day was spent at McCoy's Nursery and landscape to help Mark's sister and brother in law with their newly merged business. For two days we worked very long, very hard hours. They paid us in plants. Tomatoes and green peppers, oh boy! After we came home I worked up the garden soil and got it ready for the new plants. Within a few days I had all our little plants in their new homes. Now, if it would just rain.

I went out every morning and evening and spoke life to all the plants and flowers we had coming up in the dry heat. I sang praise songs to them. I spoke scripture verses to them. I smiled at them and blessed them each one.

As the last of June moved into early July, we had lots of fresh vegetables ready to be picked. We spread the wealth to family and friends. We were asked over and over how did we get our vegetables to grow large so fast? The weather had been so uncooperative most people couldn't get anything to grow!

I told them that all you needed was the right key to see fruit. God's key.

THE CHRISTMAS STORY LADY
ALL GOD'S PLAN
THE MAKING OF "CHRISTMAS CHAOS!"
Deborah Aubrey-Peyron

How was I ever to know that when angels walked me to the back yard of an estate sale 150 miles from my home, finding an 1863 German print of Heilige Nacht (Holy Night), the Nativity on the bottom of an old abandoned bread rack, that this was just the first leg of a journey that would span almost 17 years.

In 1995 I brought the print home for $35.00, thinking what a nice blessing it was. It was worth much more than the original $100.00 the brothers had asked for at the sale.

And to think I had argued over and over with the Lord as He told me that morning before my walk to "*take money*." I did not think I needed money. I was just going out for my usual morning walk. I did not want to go to any yard sales. I only brought $35.00 with me to get back home on. So out the door I went, penniless.

I arrived to the point where I was accustomed to turning around and heard from a heavenly unseen visitor, "*turn here.*" Argument ensued. Thankfully I lost. I acquiesced, "Okay, you obviously have an agenda. You take control of my feet, and guide me where you want me to go."

Off I went at a hurried pace! That was how I found at the back of the lot at the estate sale the beautiful picture for which the brothers wanted $100.00. This was another argument with God. "I only have $35.00!" By that time I gave in quickly and walked to the front, gathered the owners around and told them my story. I bought it for $35.00. Apparently, they were much better listeners than I was. I wondered at the time why God had set it aside just for me.

I met Mark two years later. Our relationship grew, and in less than two more years we were married and started a new blended family. As we unpacked our own belongings in the new little home Mark had purchased for our family, he found the picture. I related the story of how the picture came to me.

Within a couple of years married, the Holy Spirit prompted several people to come forward and tell us it was time to build a home. They were sure it was to be south of town. Go south west. Okay.

It was on a warm, Sunday afternoon as we drove south of town to look for land, when my husband was led by the spirit down a side road off Heidelberg. I too heard the spirit say, *"For sale by owner"* and *"$18,000.00."* We turned the curve and four houses down was our land. I knew it when I stepped onto the one and a half acre lot.

When the owner told us it was the front of Bethlehem Farms Subdivision, it did not surprise us one bit. Maybe there was a reason for the picture I bought so long ago to be in our lives. Mark had it beautifully framed as a house warming present for me and our brand new home.

Yet almost every time I passed a little side street two doors down from us, I felt an urging voice say, "You'll live back here one day." I thought it strange because I was very happy with our brand new home. In my head I planned to stay there the rest of my life. Well, so much for what I had planned. After all, they don't compare to God's plans. Sometimes, they even get in the way.

A couple of years later in our life, my back broke at the L-5, S-1. In that same home I loved, I was delivered from pain and suffering with a miraculous intervention from God. The doctor called it instantaneous regeneration. Call it what you want, I could walk and sit and stand again. Glory! Yet God chose at the time to not bless us with monetary assistance for the medical bills. We were drowning.

For two more years we struggled financially and the business I had nurtured to help patients with their medication costs, was failing. I had managed to save over 400 patients homes but could not save my own. We sold our beloved home to keep afloat. Our children cried. Partners came in and took over the business. They sold it to another company who promised better for all of us.

That was when we bought the land in back of our old home, a 10 acre lot on Nicholas Drive. We held out hope that we were being rescued. A week later my pay was stopped. I had already worked the year before with no pay. I couldn't do it again. In short order, I resigned. It could not have been worse timing. It was the beginning of the 2008 recession.

We packed "Helige Nacht" away in a box that was unopened for four very long years. In the meantime, we struggled every month just to get by. We tried to understand what had happened. Where had we gone wrong? Had we stopped listening to God? Were we being punished? The beautiful land in Bethlehem Farms on Nicholas Drive that called to our hearts, now felt like a noose around our necks. We tried a couple of times to sell it but to no avail. It felt like God Himself was sitting on our circumstances. Pastors Schuppert and Dennis told us over and over again to hold on! God was going to show Himself mighty and make something beautiful out of all this. At the time, it was way beyond my understanding.

Shortly before my 52nd birthday, God made apparent what He wanted me to do with the rest of my life. He wanted me to know I was not all washed up, and I was not through until He told me I was through! That was when word came down by different friends that I was to write all the miracles I had seen in my life and those around me.

There were patients and pastors, family members and perfect strangers who had come up one at a time saying, "I have to tell you a story. Will you remember it for me?"

"Yes, of course I will."

134 stories later, it became my first book "Miraculous Interventions™." After it was written, I sent it off to a friend to read for spelling errors.

Deborah hard at work writing
"Miraculous Interventions"

I thought my work was through. January 1, 2011 Mark and I were sitting and relaxing in the new little home in Corydon, Indiana we bought instead of building on our land. We did not have the funds to build. The land waited.

All of a sudden a story out of nowhere appeared in my head. A poem dropped in like water! I hollered, "Paper! I need paper!"

Mark jumped up and got me sheets of paper and a pen. I wrote as hard and as fast as I could for almost an hour.

My husband asked as soon as he thought it safe, "What are you doing? What are you writing?"

I laughed and said, "I don't know, but when I am finished I will read it to you." By the end of the story in poem form, "Christmas Chaos!" was born. Well, welcome to the world little story! It felt in my spirit like a "thank you" from

Heaven, but why? All the pieces to the puzzle had not been placed together yet.

I put the sweet little poem at the back of my first book not knowing what else to do with it.

In the spring of 2011 my friend Kelly Riddle had come to stay a couple of days with us for a visit. I read her the children's Christmas story, for it had no formal name yet. As she listened intently, wonderful pictures formed in her mind. She said to me, "Deb, this is meant to be a children's book."

I countered back, "Do you feel like illustrating for another author? And, can I put you on a payment plan?"

"Yes and yes!" Quick answers!

She said she would ask God what to charge me for her services. Within a couple more days, we were in business! Kelly asked me as we got started on our little project what I wanted the cover to look like.

I responded slowly, "You know, ever since I was in my 30's, the same house has been appearing to me on everything I own. A two story brick home is on my coffee cups, my drinking glasses, decanter, even a salt shaker and paper towels! I think we should use its likeness. Do you think that's why these images have been coming to me all this time?" Giggling, she nodded as she began to draw.

Miss Kelly Riddle, Illustrator

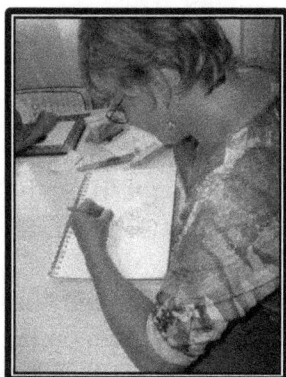

I called Mary my editor to tell her about the new project we were starting. I asked her if she would again help me produce another book. Glee squalled over the phone line, "A children's Christmas story with Christ in it! I love it!" I could always count on Mary Bibb Smith.

Kelly drew all the original delightful drawings. Mary colored the picture backgrounds with a computer program.

Deborah and Mary "bringing the illustrations to life", and having way too much fun!

Then, for over four long weeks, she and I meticulously colored each picture with colored pencils to blend them in with the backgrounds. Even my dear husband got in on the act. He drew the back cover, the back of the house itself.

By the fall of 2011 our financial circumstances fell in line well enough that we tried once again to build a home outside of town on our land on Nicholas Drive.

There had been no such thing as coincidence in my

whole life. With God's understanding, all fear about starting a new home in our 50's and what it should even look like left us. Everything was being orchestrated for God's exact time.

Glory to God!

The picture of the birth of Jesus Christ in Bethlehem that I purchased 17 years ago, getting the opportunity to buy land on Nicholas Drive in Bethlehem Farms Subdivision almost five years ago, all the pretty little two story houses on our kitchen ware that had been coming to us from various sources, and last but not least, the story that dropped in my head on January 1, 2011, all seemed to point to the same thing.

One day, I may be forever known as the writer of "Christmas Chaos!" the Christmas Story lady who lives on a small farm in Bethlehem Farms Subdivision on Nicholas Drive.

God willing.

Though the house is not built yet, the decision to build is not up to us anymore. It is where it has been all along, in God's most capable hands, just where it should be.

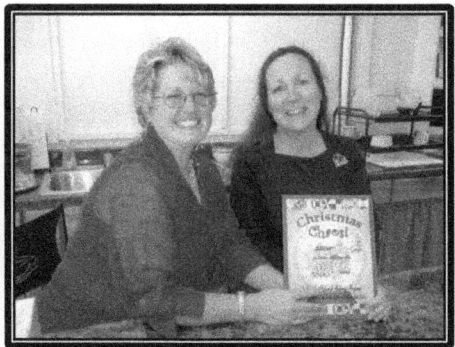

LEFT: Deb and Kelly
RIGHT: Kelly and Deb at our first book signing

Deb and Mark standing on their land on
Nicholas Drive in Bethlehem Farms,
Spring of 2012

THE LAST STORY OF 2011

During this past year we were blessed by the sale of my book to meet and make some new wonderful friends, Larry and Marilynn Crosier and Father Michael and Patti Olsen. To me, this was blessed individuals who sought out other blessed individuals.

By the end of the year our expectations were high enough and we finally felt secure enough, to apply one last time to build our home on Nicholas Drive. By then we had a good idea of what the home would look like.

We were totally surprised by what happened on January 1st, 2012. This event started a whole series of miraculous events in our lives and everyone else's around us.

But that, my dears, will be a whole new book!

Look for Miraculous Interventions:
    2012 The Miraculous Year!

God Bless and see you then!

Deb Peyron, Author

"BELIEVE"

Miraculous Interventions™ III: 2012 The Miraculous Year

By Deborah Aubrey-Peyron

A diary following the year 2012's miraculous occurrences in healing, prosperity and even through sorrows.

THE ANOINTING

The year 2011 had ended well and we looked forward to January 1st. Mark and I had already set our plans in motion. Our new good friends Larry and Marilynn Crosier had agreed to go with us to see a church in Louisville, Kentucky where the priest and his congregation were seeing angelic orbs and smelled frankincense and myrrh.

In the car I was slightly upset at the prospect of being late for mass. Not to worry, Larry driving at the helm felt no matter what my watch said, we would be right on time. And we were. It seemed the good Anglican priest, Father Mike Olsen, his wife Patti, and their congregation were also ten minutes late in starting. I am in continuous amazement of how God orchestrates the smallest of details in our lives for the benefit of our faith and trust in Him.

As Marilynn with her husband Larry, Mark and myself entered the church, we were greeted with warm smiles and 'hello's!" from Father Mike and members of his church.

Father Mike greeted us, "You're just on time! We're about to start. Have a seat." Patti, his wife was already at the piano ready to sing to the Lord! Their small congregation stood in attendance as Father Mike entered from the back of the church, with the Holy Bible and a large cross carried behind him by alter boys (or whatever they call them now). Father Mike led praise and worship before the mass officially started. He prophesied for the New Year as the Holy Spirit gave him utterance. "This is the year of angels and miracles. The war between good and evil is raging now!" (Just as I had seen in my dream years ago! That was what the angel beside me had told me!)

He quoted Jeremiah 33:3, "Call unto me, and I will

answer thee, and show thee great and mighty things, which thou knowest not." He went on, "From this rock I will build my church and the gates of hell shall not prevail against it! Dance like a child before the Lord!" What a beginning!

In my heart I asked to smell the Lord when He would be nearby. Instantly both Mark and I smelled incense. Father Mike was still before the Lord and gave more utterance. "The joy of the Lord is your strength! Release the joy! Don't be discouraged anymore! The angels are pouring out new wine! There is freedom in this place! Let me bind and heal your wounds! The enemy has no more place here in you! The work is complete! All is forgiven! Now is the time to be blessed! I am calling you to a higher place!"

Marilynn felt he was talking directly to her! God was bringing her from having a wounded spirit to new life! New friends! To a new position where she could rejoice! Marilynn felt she was back in the army of God and there was work to do! As we sang praises, I felt compelled to take pictures in the church. In almost every picture you could see many "angelic orbs". During the last part of Father Mike's prophesy before starting mass, Marilynn and I felt these words were for us. "This is the year that you break off the power that caused you harm and discouragement! No more! Let go of the words that said you were not worthy or no good!"

Then Father Mike started the mass. From the opening of the mass until after communion, the charismatic liturgy went on as expected. Larry and Marilynn enjoyed the solemnity of the service and felt the closeness of the Holy Spirit in the church.

The homily was about man. It was about man being made a little lower than the angels. All things are under his feet. We are no longer slaves but children of

God. We are heirs. Have the mind of Christ! Empty ourselves! Be obedient! Father Mike started with the gospel of Luke, and moved on to the book of Psalms, "How majestic is the name of God! See God as big as He is! His name is above all names! Call upon Jesus! Remember to plead the blood of Jesus over all your circumstances. His name is above doubt or fear. Jesus comes for His own and you are seated with Him in glory."

There is a whole other realm that the church does not address much, the supernatural realm of angels and miracles. God is here. He is above our circumstances. He is in the glory realm. Call on angels to bring you help! Plant seeds in others. With praise on our lips, we will see the manifestation of God! Praise silences your foes and enemies! Praise the Lord and watch all your enemies leave! Have a Biblical imagination! See miracles all around you! Be like Jesus! Go do the work of the Gospel. Consider what God can do. God wants us to believe from small to large. Remind God of what He has said to us in His scriptures. When we make our God big, anything is possible. Then all our problems become small."

After communion, Father Mike came forward to the front of the altar. He called out, "Someone here has back pain. Come forward to be healed."

I knew this was Marilynn's time for a full healing! I whispered, "Go! He is talking to you!"

As she walked up to the altar, Father told this story: "The oil vial I have in my hands was miraculously translated into the home of another pastor who gave it to me. The vial has a little slip of paper stating where it is from taped to it. It is miraculous oil sent to us from God."

Wow!

He anointed each person with oil from this vial. Father started to pray over Marilynn. Mark stood in back of her in case she needed to be caught. I stood beside her.

Mike told Marilynn he saw angels all around her and in her home. He had no way of knowing there were angel statues all over their house! As he prayed, her back healed instantly and she was slain in the spirit. Father Mike cried out, "God calls you daughter with a purpose for intercessory prayer!"

The next one up was Larry. He called Larry a rock. And that he should keep paper beside the bed because he was going to see angels and have angelic visitations.

"Write down what you see." Larry too, was slain in the spirit.

Father Mike then went to the other side of the church for more healing prayers. Mark got in line over there. After a few minutes it was his turn to be ministered to. It was as if he could read Mark's mind. Father Mike stated, "God has heard you. He is answering the prayers you have had in your heart right now. I see good, very good things for you. I see a new path."

With Father Mike's eyes closed standing in front of Mark, he stretched out his right arm and pointed directly at me and said, "I see radio and television interviews for you. It is all good."

He anointed several other people and then walked back to our side of the church and prayed over more people. I stood ready to catch anyone that would need it. When he finished with everyone else in line Father turned and looked at me. He said, "Well I might as well tell you too." I stood before him both hands raised to receive what he had to say.

Father Mike looked up to somewhere the natural eye couldn't see. He spoke, "I see angels on Jacob's ladder. You have God's ear this year, 2012. God has heard your cry. I see you with a wreath on your head as a crown. You are running the race. Keep running the race!

You are just getting started! You have arrived at

your destiny, your purpose in life! You will smell the angels, the very aroma of God! The Throne room! You will smell the rose of Sharon, roses and flowers. I see your boys walking closer with the Lord. God is opening doors for you both that no man can close! He will show your path clearly! Be filled with joy!"

Then Father Mike prepared and gave the final blessing to close the mass. The women all went to the kitchen to prepare the meal. The men helped take down the New Year's decorations. Father blessed the meal and we all went into fellowship.

It was then that other parishioners came forward and said they had been watching us during mass. They knew we had Catholic backgrounds because we knew all the right responses to the prayers. Our backgrounds had told on us!

All four of us helped clean up at the end of the evening. We walked out with the other parishioners taking items out to their cars for them. We were just closing Larry's trunk when I heard Father Mike calling my name and running out of St. Columba to catch us!

"Deborah! Deborah!"

"Yes Father Mike? I'm here! What is it?"

"God has spoken to me!"

"Oh my! What did our Lord have to say?"

I stood breathless waiting for his answer.

He said to me, "God said to give this miraculous oil vial to you."

I heard immediately in my spirit, "**Now it begins.**"

My knees swayed beneath me. My voice would not come out of my mouth.

I ran back to the car finally crying out, "Thank you! Thank you!" We all jumped up and down as we got in the car to head back to Mom's. All I could think of in my head was "Don't drop it, don't break it, and don't blow it.

REALLY don't blow it!"

We hadn't gotten four miles down the road when I noticed the little vial that wasn't two-thirds full had miraculously filled up and was overflowing out onto my hands! God, through this vial was anointing my hands for His work!

I shouted out to the rest of my friends in the car and told them what was happening! They could see the oil coming out of a tightly closed vial, now full to overflowing.

Immediately I knew what to do. I anointed Marilynn with oil and prayed for her ministry of intercessory prayer. Then I anointed my husband for a healing ministry. I did not anoint the driver Larry, in case he would be slain in the spirit!

Our spirits were as high as kites by the time we arrived back at Mom's. We knew when we dropped off our car earlier that she was sick with the flu. We knew what we had to do as we went into the living room. I asked if we could pray over her.

She said, "Yes, of course!"

With hands still covered in oil, we laid hands on her and prayed for her to be healed.

At the end of the prayer I did not realize that I was still under the anointing. I said to her, "Awe Mom, when we leave you are going to cough up all this goop and be just fine." Everyone laughed.

When we left, Mom coughed up all the infection. She was immediately hungry and had to eat before going to bed.

The next day she called Sandy, her daughter and told her, "I've had a miracle! I've had a miracle!"

Over the next several days, utilizing the anointing

oil, we saw physical manifestations of miracles over and over. Healings from surgeries, averting of disasters, words of knowledge, prophesies, etc...

By the third day of the new year I was told in the spirit I would be writing a third book, right along side book two. It would be called "2012 The Miraculous Year".

So be it.

IN THE BEGINNING

By Deborah Aubrey-Peyron and Mary Dow Bibb Smith

In the beginning there was always God. His plans are perfect and far exceed our plans and dreams! Though I have always been a Christian and sought the Lord, it is still wonderful to look back and see how my efforts were always part of His plan all along! As Gandalf said in *The Hobbit*, "You don't really suppose, do you, that all your adventures and escapes were managed by mere luck, just for your sole benefit? You are a very fine person, Mr. Baggins, ... but you are only quite a little fellow in a wide world after all. (Thank Goodness!)"

You see, I am a publisher, by God's grace. A beginner in the field for sure, but a publisher none the less! But, I am getting ahead of the story. And since my primary author is such a wonderful story teller, I will let her tell our story. - *Mary Smith*

"In the beginning." Such a simple way to start a story. God saw fit to start His Holy Bible with it. The meaning of the phrase showed God in the mix from the very start. The same with Mary, my best friend and publisher, and my story.

All we have ever done, all our gifts and talents, all that we have seen is now being employed for God's Holy purpose. Together we are writing the continuing "Acts of the Apostles" to encourage the brethren and inspire the secular world. How did such a daunting task occur in our lives? Why at our beginning of course!

Every good story has foreshadowing and so does ours. Fifteen years before Mary and I met, she met my younger brother, Ron at a retreat at Mt. St. Francis. I too, was supposed to have been there but, I allowed my boyfriend at the time to talk me out of going. Like Mary, I was in love with Jesus – as my Savior, brother and example on how to be a loving and forgiving human being. There was much need for that in my short life at the time. Having been hurt by man and his escapades, I knew Jesus would never hurt nor fail me. We are not going to go into great detail here. My story is already recorded in the book, *"Miraculous Interventions™"*, but we are going to give a bit of it here.

Mary and I grew up not far from one another but, on opposite sides of the Ohio River; Mary in Southern Indiana and I in Louisville, Kentucky. We have much in common. We are both charismatic Catholics, artists, mothers of three children, divorced, and "remarried" – I to my current and forever husband, Mark; and Mary has a chaste but close relationship with her former husband, Mitch.

We met in 1992 at Covenant Prayer Group at St Mary's Catholic Church in Lanesville, Indiana where we still attend. Mary was just a little ahead of me in a newly single walk. I followed three years later down that same path.

Fear not, readers! God's hand was on us even then. Happy beginnings were well on their way.

About the time Mark and I met, in 1997, God also inspired Mary to write an arts and crafts book called *Fantastic Snowflakes!* It took 12 years to complete, but it was a lifetime of love. When Mary was little her mother would have to call her in from playing outside in the snow. She loved to catch snowflakes and marveled at their structure and minute detail!

In 1st grade a memorable art project was the cutting of a paper snowflake from folded paper. Instead of becoming a beautiful snowflake the paper fell apart, she cried in disappointment! She never forgot it.

Years later Mitch, a US Army soldier, was stationed in

Germany. Mary and their twins [another miraculous story covered in *Miraculous Interventions™II*] were allowed to live there with him in Army-supplied quarters. Another child was born to them while living there as well. A U.S. friend there, knowing her love of snow, taught her how to fold the paper correctly to cut a six-sided snowflake, since all real snowflakes are six-sided – as all snowflakeologists know!

More years later at a new job with, as yet, little to do, out of boredom and with the Christmas season rapidly approaching, Mary pulled out of her bag of talents the paper snowflake. She cut so many paper snowflakes to decorate the company Christmas tree, some truly amazing ones, that people started asking her how to do it. The idea of making an instruction book was born! Then after twelve years of writing and illustrating, *Fantastic Snowflakes!* was finally ready to be published.

As good as this book was she could not get a publisher to even look at it. She set it aside.

Out of adversity the hand of God moved. Even though much had occurred in Mary's life while writing the book - her mother passed in 2002, she bought her mother's house, her ex-husband came to live with her, renting an upstairs room in her home, and she took an extra job at Office Depot in order to make ends meet, and she felt that God really wanted her to proceed with the book. A brother suggested that Mary publish it herself. This was confirmed multiple times. And since God had placed Mary at Office Depot, one of her new talents was printing and binding. Imagine that!

We were all so excited to hear of Mary's first book signing during the Christmas holidays.

Meanwhile, back at the ranch...my new husband, Mark and I were busy living life and raising three boys. Not a small task in and of itself. Occasionally in my lifetime I had been asked or assigned to write articles or stories for various schools or organizations on many topics. Writing was easy for me so I never gave it much thought more than a nice hobby. Mary and I saw each other each week at prayer group at St. Mary's. Having similar backgrounds and interests, we were naturally drawn to each other.

Mary watched as we built our first home together. She and her girls helped us move in! The preparation for our first Christmas Open House was made into a whole weekend together. My boys stayed at their father's home while the Smith's came and cooked and cleaned, hung up decorations and had a blast! For two evenings, after cooking all day, Mark would bring in dinner and we would all sit afterwards and talk of our days activities, read books, braid hair and listened to a tape of *The Twelve Days of Christmas*.

What we did not realize at the time was that God was setting in place the foundation for our destinies.

A few years after building our home in 2002, I suffered a fracture in a vertebra. It changed the direction of our lives. We had no insurance to pay for the hospital and medical bills. Mary, my friend now of 10 years, came to help take care of me while I recuperated from a procedure. Again she prepared meals in my kitchen and cleaned up after our family. We prayed and cried together at the prospect of my being an invalid, without divine intervention. Four days later, through the hands of a retired minister, I was miraculously healed! I still thank God for His mercy.

The year 2008 was pivotal not only for Mary as a start of her God-given career change, but in my life as well. As she ascended to her new goal, my life's goal at the time was being plunged into disaster. The business I had fought so hard to build to help save lives and homes, was tumultuously taken over and lost, our own home being a casualty of the battle. I had now been broken twice. I wondered, "What could God do with me now?"

"When I am weak, He is strong." I had been in battles ever since I was three days old. But I serve a God who is a rescuer of my body and my soul. He came through and spoke to my very essence. When I said, "I am all washed up. I want to die! How will my family survive this?"

God said to me, "You will live and not die. Write down everything I have ever done for you! Every miracle you have ever seen me do in your life and those around you - all the stories that have filled your life. This will help you to go on."

At the time I thought it was to save my life and for my children's sake. I wrote for two years without telling a soul, not even my husband knew. God brought back to my remembrance events from my youth, when I first heard His voice as a command to save a house from catching fire, all the way up to the present day.

As with Mary, God sent people to tell me it was "time to write the book." Wonderful. I didn't know I was writing a book. But God did. It would be a book on miracles, on God taking adversity and turning it around into blessings. I found healing and hope in its pages even as I wrote with the help of the Holy Spirit. I wondered at the time, could this book help anyone else?

As soon as I finished my manuscript, Mary was also asking God, "Okay, I did this snowflake book because I thought you wanted me to. Now what?"

At the next very Thursday prayer group meeting, I walked in, manuscript in hand. I said to my group, "Well, I have written a book and I don't know what to do with it."

Mary quickly replied, "Well, I do. I can turn it into a book for you!"

Our destinies had just joined together forever. Now we were where God wanted us to be all along.

As the book was almost ready to go to print, I was also given the gift of a beautiful little poem that just dropped into my head. It was about three unruly boys with a less-than-fortunate run-in with St. Nicholas. It was told with humor, verse, and Christ, of course! Mary was able to put it in at the end of my first book, but said it would make a good children's book all on its own if we could find a good illustrator. That very week another friend of mine who just happened to be a book illustrator, Kelly Riddle, came by for a visit.

The rest became history as we soon published a second book together called "Christmas Chaos!"

I thought surely after that we were done with all this. I must have exceeded expectations by now. Ha! As we both found out, being guided by the Holy Spirit, we were just getting started. Amazing people started dropping into my path. Stories abounded from everywhere. The next book was not so much about me and my path but about theirs. From ministers and priests, to everyday visionaries, they all came forward to boldly tell their stories so I could tell their miraculous walks of faith.

We have come to realize and believe that our story is meant for more than just us and even our area. With Pope Benedict XVI calling for 2012-2013 church year to be the "Year of Faith and Sharing," God's plans for Mary and I are certainly more than just for our "sole benefit," even though we are only "small fellow[s] in a wide world after all." As we said before, God's plans are perfect and far exceed our plans and dreams! If he can do this with us, what are His plans for you?

"For I know the plans I have for you, declares the Lord. Plans to prosper you and not to harm you, plans to give you hope and a future". (Jeremiah 29:11 NIV)

"*Miraculous Interventions*™" has now become a series with book three being written as I wrote this story. In 2012, God also brought more authors to Mary's new publishing company, *Home Crafted Artistry & Printing*, such as, Bob Garvey's book of meditations, "*Holy Spirit Tours, Winter Excursion,*" published September 2012.

By the end of 2012, our little crusade into the world of publishing has carried our books to Catholic and Protestant churches, various organizations, bookstores and public libraries in Kentucky, Indiana, Oklahoma, Texas, Pennsylvania, Washington, New York, a Federal Reformatory and the countries of England and Germany. They are also available on-line at Amazon.com.

ORDAINED BY GOD

A minor miracle occurred during the Christmas season of 2012, I was off for 12 days in a row! What a blessing! The Friday before Christmas while at Cowboy Church in Lagrange, Kentucky I mentioned this to our co-pastor, Rabbi Joy Son. She nodded and smiled. I could already see in her eyes a glint, a spark of interest! We both knew the time had come for our clandestine meeting– a 16 hour space of time away from the cares of the world to glean from one another the deep thoughts of God. Cowboy Church had an agreement with a local hotel for a special rate for their out of town guests to stay with them. Joy said she would call me when the time could be arranged.

As Christmas and the days after started flying by I began to worry about our overnight meeting. The day after Christmas I came down sick with bronchitis and double ear infections – a trip to the doctor was in order. Two days later Mark came down sick with the influenza that was wrecking havoc all over America. In all my years I had never seen my husband so ill. High temperatures and vomiting were joined by aching all over. The dear man was miserable! I surely could not leave him during his illness. I took good care of him making sure liquids stayed down and no dehydration could set in. Of course I prayed.

Then I heard from our youngest son Andy. He was going to need a baby sitter for Sam's children New Year's Eve and New Year's Day. Could I manage that as well? "Sure son." Sigh.

"Well", I thought to myself, "that's the last straw." In all these hours where I was needed by everyone else, there was only one 17 hour time frame in all those days that I could possibly get away. You got it, and I should have known all along that God was in control of the whole situation. Joy called and the only 16 hours she had free were the same 17 hours I had. Incredible.

December 30th I packed a single bag with a robe, house slippers and a gown, clothes for the next day and a few toiletries. I bought a new pad of paper with 120 sheets – just in case! I had enough money for my half of the room rate and for our dinner out. I wanted to thank Joy for her gift of time with a free meal. It was the least I could do. I made Mark his lunch and dinner, checked his temperature one more time, he was on the mend, and made sure he had my cell phone number close by. I got in the car and started on a journey that I would not come back from the same.

How can I tell you the importance of this?
Why with a story, of course...

THE WOMAN OF GOD AND THE APOSTLE

I arrived at the hotel a few minutes before Rabbi Joy Son. I went in and let the admitting clerk know I was there. When I walked back outside to gather my things Joy pulled up in her "faithful" van. I smiled and asked if I could help her bring anything in. "Yes!" A light packer she wasn't. It took a couple of trips.

Our room number was 304. We got settled in and went out to dinner – Oriental was agreed on. I drove and she led the way. I thought dinner conversation would be light and we would start our real mission when we got back to the hotel. Not necessarily so. I got to know the "woman of God" quickly during our meal. Joy spoke of some of her background and how God had called her at an early age.

She spoke of her mother and father and how very gifted they were in the spirit. No surprises there, I was getting to know their daughter's gifts rapidly.

Back at the hotel, I got out a pen and paper for our meeting. I wanted to remember everything important she had to say. But the evening didn't start with words, it started with music of a sorts and a candle. Joy put in a CD of a ship on water. You could hear the slapping of the waves against the hull. In my head it was evening. The candle crackled as we listened to the ship creak as it moved through the water towards the shore. In the distance a horn from the light house pointed the way home. She asked me if I thought they had been on a journey with great adventures. I smiled as I knew she was setting me up for a look at my own life. And hers. Was I ready to look at that adventure from another set of eyes? She had read my book. I knew revelation was at hand. I prepared to be boarded.

The first thing this woman of God wanted me to know was that I had all the same gifts she had. I could see and hear and smell beyond the veil with words of knowledge and prophesy. Yes indeed I was an emissary and an evangelist. But what I didn't have was discipline. I needed to go deeper into a relationship to hear everyday what the Lord God had to say to me. How? This was what the whole night was set up for. The how.

Joy sat quietly as I told story after story that weren't detailed in the book but felt compelled to tell her then. We sat in our pajamas with a glass of water by our side. When I was drained of all I thought important to tell, then she started ...

"Always test the voice you hear."

"Really? Can I do that?" Ignorance abounded out of my mouth before I could stop it. Rats.

"Sure you can!" Joy responded with enthusiasm.

"What about the dumb stuff He shows me? 257 pieces of gum or the color of a pastor's hair?" I wondered if those things could be important too.

"Relationship building!" she replied. Everything was becoming clearer at warp speed. "If He can trust you with small things He can trust you with big things! Test what you hear to know if it's the Holy Spirit by three ways: if it is supported in scripture, the next if it glorifies God, and the last if it edifies your spirit! This is important for your growth and development!"

Then Joy asked me a second question. "Is God male or female?" Of course, I gave the answer "male" because Jesus himself called God "Father".

Her reply gave me something to think about. Joy said, "God is male, also female. God has the characteristics of both. Strong and brave yet a loving heart. In the Hebrew and in Greek the term is masculine and feminine. The Lord God is One. It takes both the male and the female to be whole together – when we love. God calls us to a love relationship. God is whole as both. He has the

104

heart of the mother and the strength of the man."

I again asked how it is I am able to know things out of thin air sometimes. Joy's answer surprised me. "Deb", she said, "It is like Ezekiel's wheel, you see beyond the veil."

It hit me like a lightening bolt. "Wow!" "Wow!" I could scarce take it all in but it was the only thing that made complete sense. I felt unworthy to fill such big shoes. What if this were really true? Had I wasted 54 years with immature understanding? Had I let God down? This line of thought led me to a dream I had had the week before and wanted to ask her about.

"Joy, I would like to ask you to interpret a dream I had last week."

"Go ahead."

"I was in Heaven. I could see a great coliseum with white pillars. The people on stage were reenacting the life of Christ. At the end Jesus Himself appeared. He was beautiful. Once, in a vision I had seen Pastor Fred with a coat of many colors. Jesus had on the Coat of Many Nations. I automatically knew it. There were colors there I had never seen before. I saw him coming up in the stands to find me. Jesus said, "You have to be strong now! I have called you out to be strong! Your time is now!" In the dream I was afraid. Jesus called on me to have His spirit!"

Joy asked, "What season was it?"

I checked my memory and answered, "Summer, I think."

She replied, "Summer represents the end of the gentile age. It represents the harvest time."

Everything Joy revealed to me took me deeper and deeper into the supernatural world of God – out of time and into His presence. I could scarce breathe.

"We are allowed to see when we step through the veil into the Holy of Holies. Our laws and physics don't apply to God. We translate. We step through into eternity."

Joy's words hung in the air. Any words I thought of paled to this. She went on, "Cling to the one who has courage, Jesus. You are called and created for a purpose as a seer and a hearer. I am too. Step into who you are for the season is right. The deeper you trust the more you will hear and learn of the secret things of God."

I asked why is it when I am sick or down for a season I seem to hear better.

Joy answered, "We are close to the veil when we are ill or quiet, that is when we see beyond. Perspective is everything."

I asked Joy, "Have you known many seers and hearers?"

She replied, "Yes a few. Some less and some more. We glean and share from each other. God brings them. We don't seek them."

She went on, "What we have to say or think does not matter. It is obedience that matters. It is in those shared moments of obedience with God– with the presence of God and Jesus that matter."

I asked her if she had ever been in the presence of Mary, the mother of Jesus.

"No."

I offered, "I have, once, in a dream. The air went soft and the smell of a hundred flowers entered the room. I knew it was Mother Mary being introduced by a great saint that had come to tell me they were happy I wrote a book about her son, Jesus." Again I questioned, "Are people announced into Heaven?"

"Yes and no" Joy answered.

I went on, "I have heard when several people passed over. I heard when a young infant was announced. He was not announced by his first name but by his last name. The youngest male...and with another one, I'm Alive!!"

Joy answered me again, "They are announcing a celebration! They are announcing the bride to the wedding!"

"What about smells?" I quarried. "I have smelled death over people. It smells like a rotten egg. For the flesh with out the spirit is but rotten and drops off. I have also smelled the demonic coming out of a poor soul in church. I had been asked to help pray at the end of a mass with the women and I was given in the spirit what was wrong with her and the cause, which was a demonic spirit. Before I knew what I was doing I ordered it out of her in Jesus' name and it came out with a foul smell. And I have smelled when I have been visited, for example, by both of our father's. I have either smelled or heard them. Our son Andy smells when good is about to happen to people. It smells sweet to him."

Joy smiled as she replied, "You have experienced all this because you dance in and out of the veil. You can smell the scent of things on the other side too."

Joy went on, "When He wants you to notice things, He tells you." She smiled. I then told the story of the day the Lord had told me to notice a certain thing about customers while at work.

Joy responded to this quickly, "Cover yourself! Especially afterwards! So no harassment follows you! Spiritually clean your environment!"

"I will! I will!" I promised. I had done that on occasion while at work at different times, being told to immediately in the spirit, not always knowing why. I did not realize how close my enemy was there.

Joy then said, "Deb, you were created to dance in and out of the veil! Be aware and sensitive!" Then she spoke of both of us, "Gifts are placed in us and occasionally an anointing on top of it." I remembered the anointing that fell on me when Pastor Fred prayed over me the first time. He said it was virtue. Power. At the time, I had little understanding of what that meant.

Joy prayed quietly in her heart and then said, "God has said to tell you My goodness will walk before you. Deb, this is the presence of God's goodness. He tells us goodness and mercy follow us all our days. So, what is goodness; it is virtue, truth, forgiveness and all together they equal power. It will come on you not as a washing but as a mantle resting on you. This is beyond just truth or forgiveness. The virtue of God is interchanged with goodness. For example, goodness walked before Abraham and Moses. It is a characteristic of God. You have heard God in different ways throughout your life and at different times. Have a talk with Him. He will encourage you to go on."

Joy then began to tell some of her story so I could relate to what she had told me. Her first encounter with God's voice was at eight years old. By the age of nine she was in the presence of the Lord God. Joy could hear the Holy Spirit and converse with Him. She appreciated her angels and prayed for them to have strength for their job. But her real relationship was with the Holy Spirit, - the Promised One.

I asked, "Could I be calling the voice I hear, angels, really be the Holy Spirit?"

Joy replied quickly, "Yes! He wants you to know His voice. You are called to hear. Angels are designed for a purpose. The Holy Spirit is a person of God. He is the Promised One-He sits above the angels for us to have a relationship with."

I commented, "One time, a long time ago, I was shown it this way; God as the proper noun, the Holy Spirit as a verb or action word, and Jesus as the adjective."

Smiling Joy said, "That would make the veil a

prepositional phrase!"

Now we were both in on it! Silliness abounded as laughter ensnared both of us! Joy went on, "Knowing is a gift of God. It appears with no explanation. Always test and share what you hear. Remember laughter confuses the enemy – he doesn't know what to do with it. He wants to keep us down."

I told Joy, "Andy is good with laughter! It is one of his best gifts!"

"Jesus came to give a face to God." I nodded in agreement.

"Blessed is He who comes in the name of the Lord!" Joy proclaimed. "He is our specific intercessor. And you are called to be a general." My breath left me. I had been named at birth, Deborah Anne, the Old Testament and the New Testament. Deborah was a judge and a general for the Israelites. St. Anne was Mary's mother. Had my own mother named me rightly from my very beginning? With her words, Joy taught me about myself, "Prior to 2013, it has been important for you to develop and share your story. You are an emissary and an evangelist. But, for such a time that is to come...what you were really created for, God needed to fine tune and discipline His General – for you to become. Until now, you have been in military school."

"Yes!!" A light had been lit.

"You have encountered gifts and an anointing. You have been brought here to disciple and others will glean from you and with you."

"Dear Lord, may I be up to the tasks that You have at hand for me."

Joy's father, Jim Chambers had studied with Katherine Kuhlman and had helped start New Covenant Fellowship. Joy studied under great prophets, and generals from the time she was a little girl. Her father was the "blind prophet." She asked me about some of the people

God had recently placed in my path to help me.

The story became an Ezekiel's Wheel.

*Vicki Sampson had been my best friend for 38 years. Her son, Gary, was my boyfriend all through high school. She asked me to come to a TOPS meeting to speak about nutrition health in the spring of 2011. (Taking Off Pounds Sensibly)

*At the same time, Gary looked for a writer's group in Louisville for me. He found a phone number for me to call, which I did. They gave me the date for the next meeting. The president would not be there but I could still visit. I went but my work was not well received – they were a secular group. When the president came back from vacation the next week, she called me. It was she that gave me the name and phone number of Louisville Christian Writer's President, Crystal Murray.

* The day I went to speak at TOPS was the first and only class that Fr. Mike and Patti Olsen came to. After class Fr. Mike came up and said, "You're charismatic! The Holy Spirit told me!" He was the pastor of an Anglican Church where they were seeing angelic orbs! Our first night to go to mass there, January 1st, 2012 the Lord told Father Mike to give me miraculous oil for my healing ministry. (My healing ministry?)

*At dinner after the TOPS meeting, Jim and Ann Carter, revealed to me Jim had been prayed over by the Hunter's Group – the same group that had prayed over Lee Schwarz, husband to my chemistry professor in nursing school in 1998 – given healing ability– who healed my broken back in December 2004. A second disciple from the group dealing daily in the miraculous! Could this go back any further?

*I called LCW, left my name and phone number with a mention of my books.

I received a call back from Crystal two hours later.

During that time, she had looked me up, looked up my books, and what they and I were all about. Within ten minutes we were fast friends– soon to be sisters in Christ Jesus. That was when she said to me, "You deal in miracles. You have anointing in your hands. I am bringing my sister from Arizona here and she is going to get healed! And by the way, our next meeting is in a couple of weeks. Please attend." As if it were really up to me. By that time, God was showing way off!

*Before the meeting with LCW and the official meeting of Crystal and her husband David, we invited Fr. Mike and Patti over for dinner. During the conversation I asked them how they had come to live in this area after living all over the world. They said in the middle 1990's they were approached by a Mennonite group they associated with to come and help a lady doctor who was dying of cancer in Louisville. She was my children's pediatrician, and if I hadn't been going through a horrible divorce at the time, I would have been considered for what ended up being their position. They took my place in caring for a dear friend.

*At the end of spring 2012, four days before Crystal, her sister, and David came over for dinner, we had a realtor over to find out how much our house appraised for. He told us and said we couldn't afford to have him sell it. When he left I asked God what to do now and He said, **"I have already sold your home."**

"Okay."

Four days later over dessert Crystal said for us to take our sign down– they were going to buy our home. By the way, how much did we want for it? Warp speed.

*Once the relationship with Crystal and David had been established, she wanted Mark and I to come to "Cowboy Days" in LaGrange, Kentucky to meet a friend of hers.

We had two other things planned for that same day. I made excuses not to go. The day before that meeting at the end of June, 2012, the Murray's came for a visit with Mark. I got off late that evening and they were still at our home visiting. Crystal looked at me and said, "I want you to meet my friend, Joy. She sees angels and demons. She can see inside people. She talks to God and He talks back." I got up from my chair, went into the kitchen, pulled out both calendars, struck off both events and penciled in "Cowboy Days with the Murray's."

*The next day we met Crystal and her family in LaGrange. We were warmly greeted by several in the group and then taken to meet Pastor Zeb and his wife, Joy. Crystal introduced me to Joy. Joy looked up from what she was doing, studied me, looked all around me, then, she smiled at me and said, "Hello." Joy was told along time ago in the spirit that she would meet 9 people on this earth who had all the gifts she had.

She was on number six. I was number seven. The Holy Spirit told her I was number seven and that one day soon, we would have time together and she would answer all the questions I had from all my life– and ready me to be a general in the Army of God.

By the time we got to the end of this wheel my head was reeling! For 27 years God had been turning events for this very moment. Joy said it was for validation and perspective – so we could know that God sees and orchestrates finite details for such a time as this and is to come. Count on God.

Joy asked me if I knew who Lester Summerall was. I had heard of him. He had learned from Smith Wigglesworth himself. She had great respect for his faith and gleaned from him. She built her own faith on that foundation. With all the people we had been associated

112

with in our lifetime, she and I felt honored, blessed and unworthy. Who were we? Everything else in this world was small and finite. Our days here are a blessing and a gift – not more than that.

That morning the Holy Spirit had told Joy that I am a seer, a hearer and all I needed was discipline to become a general. I was not prepared yet. It would be a validation for me to know who Joy was.

Joy was and is a people's prophet. She was prophesied over in the 1990's that her mantle was a vest of many colors. What the Lord needs in any given moment, that anointing would fall on her at that time. (I have lived this too!) She wouldn't excel at just one thing – she would flow in and out of the gifts! She was an open and pliable vessel. And so was I. Joy said, "God waits for us on the other side of those moments–what ever that moment is. When we get on the other side of the moment, God is waiting and proud of us. He waits to thank us."

"Open me up and pour me out!" I cried. This was action packed.

"Yes time is short. Perilous times are soon to come," Joy said softly.

Then Joy addressed something near and dear to my heart, our home on Nicholas Drive, yet to be constructed at that time. She said "The house is an illusion for something more that God wants to do in that place. Don't worry, God uses illusions. What looks like an unsafe venture to one person may be security to someone else. God has a plan – hang onto that. It is God's plan and His time. All is perspective. You are not going to be home until you are on the other side of the veil. When you sold or built homes for others, you were building lives. The land is not home. What ever you build, is not home. Home is on the other side. Every step you have taken for the last twenty years has been investing in that. The land is here for a purpose.

It is for a refuge. God calls it a safe place, or a place of safety. Don't mix what you are seeing in the spirit with what you see in the flesh. What is in the flesh is the illusion for safe refuge. You have two different puzzles you are mixing together."

Joy stopped so I could take in what she had told me. She listened for a voice that I could not hear. Then she began to speak again, "You are grieving for this! You must be pliable in order to be a general. You set deadlines for God. God sees deadlines differently than we do. You know He works best in the eleventh hour! After all, that's when He gets to show off a miracle! Be mindful of Him and what He is doing. Listen when you need to do something. No longer let this consume you. Separate your puzzle pieces." Joy listened again and said, "The land and the home on Nicholas Drive are resources to provide for you when you need it. The cavern is an important find. The house there will be to meet an ends. It is also to provide a safe place – for those who will need it when you and Mark go home." (Rapture) "The eleventh hour is not here yet."

Then we spoke of the Rapture to be. I said, "When the Holy Spirit is called up, all who are holy, spirit-filled, must go up as well. We cannot be split up from our spirit. Is this why there must be a rapture, when God's spirit leaves the earth, all who are attached to it must leave as well?" Wisdom was setting in. Joy nodded, "Yes."

Joy spoke about my husband, "Mark is a treasured gift. God kisses him all the time but he doesn't recognize it sometimes." She asked me a question, "When disappointments happen, what do you do with them?" Perplexed, I shook my head.

"They can bring you closer to God or you can get bitter about it. God reminds you of the opportunity of choice – to choose between God or bitterness – then it can

114

become a gift. His ways are not our ways." It was hard to hear her at that point, I sobbed as though I was one without comfort.

I asked, "How does this help my husband?"

Joy replied, "Mark is seeing through exhaustion and sickness right now. This is where his perspective is. He cannot base any decision on how he feels right now."

The conversation came back around to us.

"God sees you as more than what you walk in currently. Mark has insecurities. He is a man of velvet and a man of steel. He walks in two worlds. He is sold out to God! But Mark's insecurity hangs onto what he can see and touch. He needs to let go. When he does, there will be no limit. God sees him as so much more. Mark questions whether he sees or hears even when he does. In his exhaustion, Mark grabs hold of the nearest thing he thinks will help. And all along, God is talking to his heart."

By the late evening, with all my questions asked, my stories told and my tears counted, I had poured out enough to be able to receive what I was really there for – validation – on all that I had seen and heard. Joy told of her walk with God so I would know who it was that was speaking to me and how God had made her to be a pliable vessel with all the gifts poured into her, so she could pour them back out to help others. And what a walk that was.

Like mine, she had started young hearing the holy spirit call her name. One night, an angel appeared in her room. The angel told her, "Take my hand." Joy looked down and saw her body. The next thing she knew she was in a part of Heaven. She felt the warmth of a love so deep surround her and overtake her. As she was standing next to the angel, Joy could hear the voice of God from the Throne Room. He told her He loved her and that she had a purpose. *"Go back. You have a lot to do."*

"I don't want to leave!" the little girl sobbed.

God spoke again, *"I have created you for this. I will always love you and never leave you."*

Joy again took the angel's hand and was led back into her body. Things have never been the same since.

As the years went by the Holy Spirit accelerated her learning! Visions, seeing and hearing were her gifts. Words of knowledge appeared in her head at God's will.

At the first of every year, Joy would ask for a word for that year. In 2011, the same year I was told to make my manuscript into a book, she too was told to open up and share with people. Just as God had a word for me, *"discipline"*, God also had a word for her, *"stay focused."* Joy saw herself in a vision climbing a high mountain, at the top was God's presence. She was going up for a promotion. The Lord showed her there would be others coming up behind her that she would need to encourage.

I was sure one of those was me. "Why now?"

"Because generals are needed now! Remember, these are perilous times. People have to grow up in the spirit and step into who they are called to be. All are called. Yet not all will come." God told Joy, *"When I bring them to you, make disciples of them."*

It was almost midnight. I was weary from our talk together, speaking deep conversations about God. Joy got up off the couch and rummaged through the bag she had brought with her. She took out a plastic container and went into the bathroom. I could hear her running water. Joy came back with a towel over her shoulder and water in the container. She sat me in a chair in front of her. Joy went to her knees, and I sobbed great tears as she washed and anointed my feet. She quoted Holy Scripture, and prayed over me for my journey.

"Now it begins."

I started on this journey 50 years ago as a child, then a student, as an adult, an evangelist, an emissary, a messenger, and an author. Now, a modern day apostle. How can I tell you with mere words the power that was exchanged in that moment in time?

She gave the container to me.

"There is certain responsibility and effort required on our part. We can go to the person of the Holy Spirit and ask for understanding. He will reveal God to you, in you and through you. Say each day, 'Holy Spirit, I invite you into my day.' Establish a relationship with Him. He will show you who you are. Listen when He tells you something or something to do and respond to it!"

In the early hours of the morning I heard my name called with urgency, "Debbie!" On awakening later that same morning Joy heard with her ears, "Joy!" It was the Holy Spirit that had called each of us! He was letting us know He was nearby and in the mix. Over breakfast Joy shared, "When you hear, ask and make sure of what you heard. Start a conversation. Know the voice that calls you to attention. We are called to be seers, hearers, knowers, and have understanding. Cast down all vain imaginations! Don't let a negative seed thought grab you and run! As a creative minded person, you are susceptible. This will be difficult for you and it will take effort to defeat it. Don't give the dark side any credence. We have a higher accountability. And just because you can, doesn't mean you should."

Joy ended the conversation with this thought, "By the way, where you are working now is only temporary. God showed this to me six or eight weeks back. Don't worry about it."

"Okay."

Okay.

*"**Who** shall separate us*
from the love of Christ?
Shall tribulation, or distress,
or persecution, or famine,
or nakedness, or peril, or sword?

***Nay,** in all these things*
we are more than conquerors
through Him that loved us.
For I am persuaded that
neither death, or life
nor angels, nor principalities,
nor powers, nor things present,
nor things to come,
nor height, nor depth,
nor any other creature,
shall be able to separate us
from the love of God,
which is in
Christ Jesus Our Lord."

Romans 8:35, 37-39

Christmas Chaos!

by Deborah Aubrey-Peyron

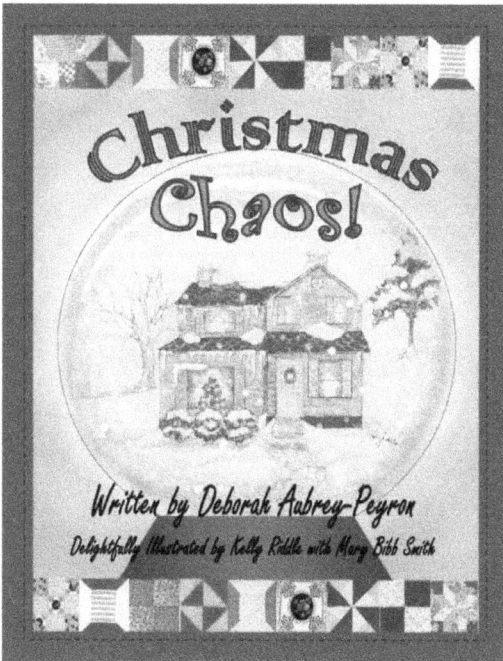

Delightlfully Illustrated by Kelly Riddle with **Mary Bibb Smith, the author Deborah Aubrey-Peyron** and **Mark Peyron**

Actual book is in full color.

A family with three unruly boys have a less-than-fortunate run-in with St. Nicholas.

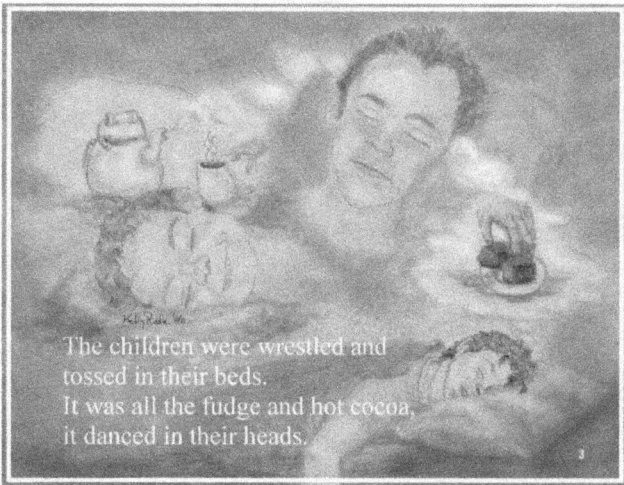

The children were wrestled and tossed in their beds.
It was all the fudge and hot cocoa,
it danced in their heads.

But our order's were clear,
up to their bedroom's we'd send,

and have to figure out,
how all this, we would amend.

This is a delightfully illustrated children's Christmas story told with humor, verse, and Christ, of course. A fun story sure to become a Christmas family tradition!

We brought him inside
and setting him down,
"No more chimneys tonight my friend,
we're your last stop in this little town!"

"Our Jesus in the Bible,
Tells us all true,
That He lived and died for us,
For me and for you.

The stories in these books have been written in order to encourage the brethren and inspire the secular world.

To contact the author, Deborah Aubrey-Peyron via email:

peyronsinjesus@yahoo.com

To contact the publisher Mary Dow Smith via email:

HomeCraftedArtistry@yahoo.com

or by mail to:

Home Crafted Artistry & Printing
1252 Beechwood Avenue
New Albany, IN 47150

ISBN 13 Numbers for the Books:

"Sample Book of the Miraculous Interventions™ Series of Books"   **ISBN-13: 978 0 9893714 0 7**

"Miraculous Interventions™
   ISBN-13: 978 0 9827621 6 5

"Miraculous Interventions™II: Modern Day Priests, Prophets, Pastors And Everyday Visionaries"
ISBN 13: 978 0 9827621 9 6

"Miraculous Interventions™III: 2012 The Miraculous Year"   **ISBN 13: 978 0 9893714 1 4**

"Christmas Chaos!" **ISBN-13: 978 0 9827621 3 4**

www.ingramcontent.com/pod-product-compliance
Lightning Source LLC
Chambersburg PA
CBHW020505030426
42337CB00011B/239